# SCOTTISH HARVEST

# SCOTTISH HARVEST

*An Anthology of Scottish Prose*
*compiled by*
ISABEL F. McPHEDRAN, M.A.
*and*
F. PHILIP KITCHEN, M.A.
*Coatbridge High School*

BLACKIE AND SON LIMITED
LONDON AND GLASGOW

BLACKIE & SON LIMITED
5 FITZHARDINGE STREET · LONDON · W1
BISHOPBRIGGS · GLASGOW

BLACKIE & SON (INDIA) LIMITED
103-5 FORT STREET · BOMBAY

PRINTED IN GREAT BRITAIN AT THE PRESS OF THE PUBLISHER

# PREFACE

THIS BOOK AIMS at presenting for secondary schools a selection of passages in prose that are essentially Scottish in character. The authors from whom we have drawn, ranging from earlier to contemporary names, are of Scottish birth, or at least Scottish by adoption; the scene is Scotland; and it is hoped above all that the particular character of the land and people, the spirit of Scotland, is always present.

In choosing the passages, no attempt was made to include all the notable names among Scottish prose-writers; and, in fact, some pieces were selected for their own merit, interest, or theme, rather than for the name at their head, so long as they represented an aspect of the subject which it was felt should be included. The scene ranges from the Borders to the Highlands, from the urbanized belt of central Scotland to the farming lands of the north-east corner, although, of course, each region may not be equally represented. Industrial Scotland, for example, does not figure prominently. The reason is obvious. The character and hence the literature of one industrialized community approximates in many ways to that of any other and national traits are much less clearly marked.

The contents are arranged under six heads: fact and fiction of former times by earlier writers; fact and fiction of former times by present day writers; and fact and fiction of today by present-day writers. The topics, which are as varied as those very broad lines allow, are not arranged chronologically within their sections but rather according to their subject-matter. It is hoped, however, that a fair unity will be found in each piece, and yet that the passages will serve as an introduction to further reading. A map is included for reference.

The collection is intended to appeal to Scots in particular, but not to them only. We hope it may give the general reader and the visitor to Scotland some insight into our Scottish ways. We hope too, that, in view of the increasing awareness of things Scottish being encouraged by the Scottish Education Department, young Scots in school and out may find pleasure and further interest in the land of their birth.

I. F. Mc P.
F. P. K.

# ACKNOWLEDGMENTS

THE EDITORS and publishers make grateful acknowledgment to the following for permission to include in this book copyright material from the works named:

The author and Messrs. William Heinemann, Ltd., for the extract from *Scottish Journey* by Edwin Muir.

The author and Serif Books, Ltd., for the extract from *Apprentice Majesty* by Agnes Mure Mackenzie.

The Tweedsmuir Estate and Messrs. John Lane The Bodley Head, Ltd., for the extract from *John Burnet of Barns* by John Buchan.

Messrs. Thomas Nelson & Sons, Ltd., for the extract from *Stories of the Border Marches* by John and Jean Lang.

The author for the extract from *Hatter's Castle* by A. J. Cronin.

The author and Messrs. William Collins, Sons & Co., Ltd., for the extract from *The Constant Star* by George Blake.

The author and Messrs. Gerald Duckworth and Co., Ltd., for the extract from *Return to Scotland* by Moray McLaren.

The Porpoise Press and Messrs. Faber & Faber, Ltd., for the extract from *My Scotland* by William Power; the author and Messrs. Faber for the extract from *Highland Pack* by Neil M. Gunn; and the author and Messrs. Faber for the story *The Dancers* by Eric Linklater.

Messrs. G. Bell & Sons, Ltd., for the extract from *Island Years* by F. Fraser Darling; and for the extract from *Quest by Canoe* by Alastair M. Dunnett.

Messrs. Robert Hale, Ltd., for the extract from *The North-east Lowlands of Scotland* by John R. Allan; and for the extract from *The Highlands of Scotland* by Seton Gordon.

Messrs. Frederick Muller, Ltd., for the extract from *The Glasgow Story* by Colm Brogan.

The author for the extract from *Always a Little Further* by Alastair Borthwick.

Messrs. Hutchinson & Co., Ltd., for the extract from *Dancing in the Streets* by Clifford Hanley.

The author and Messrs. Constable & Co., Ltd., for the extract from *Wax Fruit* by Guy McCrone.

Messrs. John Murray, Ltd., for the extract from *Seen and Heard* by Jane H. Findlater.

Messrs. Jarrolds, Ltd., for the extract from *Sunset Song* by Lewis Grassic Gibbon.

Messrs. William Blackwood & Sons, Ltd., for the extract from *Para Handy Tales* and for the extract from *The Lost Pibroch*, both by Neil Munro.

The Lutterworth Press for the extract from *String Lug the Fox* by David Stephen.

Messrs. Gerald Duckworth & Co., Ltd., for the extract from *The Campaigns of Captain MacGurk* by Robert Kemp.

# CONTENTS

# CONTENTS

---

# SCOTLAND YESTERDAY

## FACT

---

# JAMES BOSWELL

## STORM OFF MULL

. . * . .

WHILE we were chatting in the indolent style of men who were to stay here all this day at least, we were suddenly roused at being told that the wind was fair, that a little fleet of herring-busses was passing by for Mull, and that Mr. Simpson's vessel was about to sail. Hugh M'Donald, the skipper, came to us, and was impatient that we should get ready, which we soon did. Dr. Johnson, with composure and solemnity, repeated the observation of Epictetus, that, 'as man has the voyage of death before him—whatever may be his employment, he should be ready at the master's call; and an old man should never be far from the shore, lest he should not be able to get himself ready.' He rode, and I and the other gentlemen walked, about an English mile to the shore, where the vessel lay. Dr. Johnson said he should never forget Skye, and returned thanks for all civilities. We were carried to the vessel in a small boat which she had, and we set sail very briskly about one o'clock. I was much pleased with the motion for many hours. Dr. Johnson grew sick, and retired under cover, as it rained a good deal. I kept above, that I might have fresh air, and finding myself not affected by the motion of the vessel, I exulted in being a stout seaman, while Dr. Johnson was quite in a state of annihilation. But I was soon humbled; for often imagining that I could go with ease to America or the East Indies, I became very sick, but kept above board, though it rained hard.

As we had been detained so long in Skye by bad weather, we gave up the scheme that Coll had planned for us of visiting several islands, and contented ourselves with the prospect of seeing Mull, and Icolmkill and Inchkenneth, which lie near to it.

Mr. Simpson was sanguine in his hopes for a while, the wind being fair for us. He said he would land us at Icolmkill that night. But when the wind failed, it was resolved we should make for the Sound of Mull, and land in the harbour of Tobermory. We kept near the five herring vessels for some time; but afterwards four of them got before us, and one little wherry fell behind us. When we got in full view of the point of Ardnamurchan, the wind changed, and was directly against our getting into the Sound. We were then obliged to tack, and get forward in that tedious manner. As we advanced, the storm grew greater, and the sea very rough. Coll then began to talk of making for Eigg, or Canna, or his own island. Our skipper said he would get us into the Sound. Having struggled for this a good while in vain, he said he would push forward until we were near the land of Mull, where we might cast anchor, and lie till the morning; for although, before this, there had been a good moon, and I had pretty distinctly seen not only the land of Mull, but up the Sound, and the country of Morven as at one end of it, the night was now grown very dark. Our crew consisted of one M'Donald, our skipper, and two sailors, one of whom had but one eye; Mr. Simpson himself, Coll, and Hugh M'Donald his servant, all helped. Simpson said he would willingly go for Coll, if young Coll or his servant would undertake to pilot us to a harbour; but, as the island is low land, it was dangerous to run upon it in the dark. Coll and his servant appeared a little dubious. The scheme of running for Canna seemed then to be embraced; but Canna was ten leagues off, all out of our way; and they were afraid to attempt the harbour of Eigg. All these different plans were successively in agitation. The old skipper still tried to make for the land of Mull; but then it was considered that there was no place there where we could anchor in safety. Much time was lost in striving against the storm. At last it became so rough, and

threatened to be so much worse, that Coll and his servant took
more courage, and said they would undertake to hit one of the
harbours in Coll.—'Then let us run for it, in God's name,' said
the skipper; and instantly we turned towards it. The little
wherry which had fallen behind us had hard work. The master
begged that, if we made for Coll, we should put out a light to
him. Accordingly one of the sailors waved a glowing peat for
some time. The various difficulties that were started, gave me a
good deal of apprehension, from which I was relieved, when I
found we were to run for a harbour before the wind. But my
relief was but of short duration; for I soon heard that our sails
were very bad, and were in danger of being torn in pieces, in
which case we should be driven upon the rocky shore of Coll. It
was very dark and there was a heave and incessant rain. The
sparks of the burning peat flew so much about, that I dreaded the
vessel might take fire. Then, as Coll was a sportsman, and had
powder on board, I figured that we might be blown up. Simpson
and he appeared a little frightened, which made me more so;
the perpetual talking, or rather shouting, which was carried on
in Erse, alarmed me still more. A man is always suspicious of
what is saying in an unknown tongue; and, if fear be his passion at
the time, he grows more afraid. Our vessel often lay so much on
one side, that I trembled lest she should be overset, and indeed
they told me afterwards that they had run her sometimes to
within an inch of the water, so anxious were they to make what
haste they could before the night should be worse. I now saw
what I never saw before, a prodigious sea, with immense billows
coming upon a vessel, so as that it seemed hardly possible to
escape. There was something grandly horrible in the sight. I am
glad I have seen it once. Amidst all these terrifying circumstances
I endeavoured to compose my mind. It was not easy to do it; for
all the stories that I had heard of the dangerous sailing among the
Hebrides, which is proverbial, came full upon my recollection.
When I thought of those who were dearest to me, and would

suffer severely, should I be lost, I upbraided myself, as not having a sufficient cause for putting myself in such danger.

It was half an hour after eleven before we set ourselves in the course for Coll. As I saw them all busy doing something, I asked Coll, with much earnestness, what I could do. He, with a happy readiness, put into my hand a rope, which was fixed to the top of one of the masts, and told me to hold it till he bade me pull. If I had considered the matter, I might have seen that this could not be of the least service; but his object was to keep me out of the way of those who were busy working the vessel, and at the same time to divert my fear, by employing me, and making me think that I was of use. Thus did I stand firm to my post, while the wind and rain beat upon me, always expecting a call to pull my rope.

The man with one eye steered; old M'Donald, and Coll and his servant, lay upon the fore-castle, looking sharp out for the harbour. It was necessary to carry much cloth, as they termed it, that is to say, much sail, in order to keep the vessel off the shore of Coll. This made violent plunging in a rough sea. At last they spied the harbour of Lochiern, and Coll cried, 'Thank God, we are safe!' We ran up till we were opposite to it, and cast anchor.

Dr. Johnson had all this time been quiet and unconcerned. He had lain down on one of the beds, and having got free from his sickness, was satisfied. The truth is, he knew nothing of the danger we were in.

There was in the harbour, before us, a Campbeltown vessel, the *Betty*, Kenneth Morison master, taking in kelp, and bound for Ireland. We sent our boat to beg beds for two gentlemen, and that the master would send his boat, which was larger than ours. He accordingly did so, and Coll and I were accommodated in his vessel till the morning.

*from* THE JOURNAL OF A TOUR TO THE HEBRIDES

# ALEXANDER SMITH

## LOCH CORUISK

. . * . .

Picking your steps carefully over huge boulder and slippery stone, you come upon the most savage scene of desolation in Britain. Conceive a large lake filled with dark green water, girt with torn and shattered precipices; the bases of which are strewn with ruin since an earthquake passed that way, and whose summits jag the sky with grisly splinter and peak. There is no motion here save the white vapour steaming from the abyss. The utter silence weighs like a burden upon you; you feel an intruder in the place. The hills seem to possess some secret; to brood over some unutterable idea which you can never know. You cannot feel comfortable at Loch Coruisk, and the discomfort arises in a great degree from the feeling that you are outside everything—that the thunder-splitten peaks have a life with which you cannot intermeddle. The dumb monsters sadden and perplex. Standing there, you are impressed with the idea that the mountains are silent because they are listening so intently. And the mountains are listening, else why do they echo our voices in such a wonderful way? Shout here like an Achilles in the trenches. Listen! The hill opposite takes up your words, and repeats them one after another, and curiously tries them over with the gravity of a raven. Immediately after, you hear a multitude of skyey voices.

'Methinks that there are spirits among the peaks.'

How strangely the clear strong tones are repeated by these granite precipices! Who could conceive that Horror had so sweet a voice! Fainter and more musical they grow; fainter, sweeter, and more remote, until at last they come on your ear as if from the blank of the sky itself. McIan fired his gun, and it reverberated in a whole battle of Waterloo. We kept the hills busy with shouts and the firing of guns, and then McIan led us to a convenient place for lunching. As we trudge along something lifts itself off a rock—'tis an eagle. See how grandly the noble creature soars away. What sweep of wings! What a lord of the air! And if you cast up your eyes you will see his brother hanging like a speck beneath the sun. Under McIan's guidance, we reached the lunching-place, unpacked our basket, devoured our fare, and then lighted our pipes and smoked—in the strangest presence. Thereafter we bundled up our things, shouldered our guns, and marched in the track of ancient Earthquake towards our boat. Embarked once again and sailing between the rocky portals of Loch Scavaig, I said, 'I would not spend a day in that solitude for the world. I should go mad before evening.'

*from* A SUMMER IN SKYE

## JOHN BROWN

### QUEEN MARY'S CHILD GARDEN

· · * · ·

IF any one wants a pleasure that is pleasure to please, one for which he needn't growl the sardonic beatitude of the great Dean, let him, when the Mercury is at 'Fair', take the 9 a.m. train to the North, and a return ticket for Callander, and when he arrives at Stirling, let him ask the most obliging and knowing of stationmasters to telegraph to 'the Dreadnought' for a carriage to be in waiting. When passing Dunblane Cathedral, let him

(H 448)

resolve to write to the *Scotsman*, advising the removal of a couple of shabby trees which obstruct the view of that beautiful triple end-window which Mr. Ruskin and everybody else admires, and by the time he has written this letter in his mind, and turned the sentences to it, he will find himself at Callander and the carriage all ready. Giving the order for the Port of Monteith, he will rattle through this hard-featured, and to our eye, comfortless village, lying ugly amid so much grandeur and beauty, and let him stop on the crown of the bridge, and fill his eyes with the perfection of the view up the Pass of Leny, the Teith lying diffuse and asleep, as if its heart were in the Highlands and it were loth to go, the noble Ben Ledi imaged in its broad stream. Then let him make his way across a bit of pleasant moor-land—flushed with maiden-hair and white with cotton-grass, and fragrant with the Orchis conopsia, well deserving its epithet 'odoratissima'.

He will see from the turn of the hillside the Blair of Drummond waving with corn and shadowed with rich woods where eighty years ago there was a black peat-moss; and far off, on the horizon, Damyat and the Touch Fells; and at his side the little loch of Ruskie, in which he may see five Highland cattle, three tawny brown and two brindled, standing in the still water—themselves as still, all except their swishing tails and winking ears—the perfect images of quiet enjoyment. By this time he will have come in sight of the Lake of Monteith, set in its woods, with its magical shadows and soft gleams. There is a loveliness, a gentleness and peace about it more like 'lone St. Mary's Lake', or Derwent Water, than of any of its sister lochs. It is lovely rather than beautiful, and is a sort of gentle prelude, in the minor key, to the coming glories and intenser charms of Loch Ard and the true Highlands beyond.

You are now at the Port, and have passed the secluded and cheerful manse, and the parish kirk with its graves, close to the lake, and the proud aisle of the Grahams of Gartmore washed by its waves. Across the road is the modest little inn, a Fisher's

Tryst. On the unruffled water lie several isles, plump with rich foliage, brooding like great birds of calm. You sometimes think of them as on, not in, the lake, or like clouds lying in a nether sky—'like ships waiting for the wind'. You get a coble, and a yauld[1] old Celt, its master, and are rowed across to Inch-mahome, the Isle of Rest. Here you find on landing huge Spanish chestnuts, one lying dead, others standing stark and peeled, like gigantic antlers, and others flourishing in their viridis senectus, and in a thicket of wood you see the remains of a monastery of great beauty, the design and workmanship exquisite.

You wander through the ruins, overgrown with ferns and Spanish filberts and old fruit-trees, and at the corner of the old monkish garden you come upon one of the strangest and most touching sights you ever saw—an oval space of about eighteen feet by twelve, with the remains of a double row of boxwood all round, the plants of box being about fourteen feet high, and eight or nine inches in diameter, healthy, but plainly of great age.

What is this? It is called in the guide-books Queen Mary's Bower; but besides its being plainly not in the least a bower, what could the little Queen, then five years old, and 'fancy free', do with a bower? It is plainly, as was, we believe, first suggested by our keen-sighted and diagnostic Professor of Clinical Surgery, the Child Queen's Garden, with her little walk, and its rows of boxwood left to themselves for three hundred years. Yes, without doubt, 'here is that first garden of her simpleness'. Fancy the little, lovely, royal child, with her four Marys, her playfellows, her child maids of honour, with their little hands and feet, and their innocent and happy eyes, pattering about that garden all that time ago, laughing, and running, and gardening as only children do and can. As is well known, Mary was placed by her mother in this Isle of Rest before sailing from the Clyde for France. There is something 'that tirls[2] the heartstrings a'' to the life' in standing and looking on this unmistakeable living relic

---

[1] sturdy          [2] stirs, draws

of that strange and pathetic old time. Were we Mr. Tennyson, we would write an Idyll of that child Queen, in that garden of hers, eating her bread and honey, getting her teaching from the holy men, the monks of old, and running off in wild mirth to her garden and her flowers, all unconscious of the black lowering thunder-cloud on Ben Lomond's shoulder.

You have ample time to linger there amid 'the gleams, the shadows, and the peace profound', and get your mind informed with quietness and beauty, and fed with thoughts of other years, and of her whose story, like Helen of Troy's, will continue to move the hearts of men as long as the grey hills stand round about that gentle lake, and are mirrored at evening in its depths. You may do and enjoy all this, and be in Princes Street by 9 p.m.; and we wish we were as sure of many things as of your saying 'Yes, this is a pleasure that has pleased, and will please again; this was something expected that did not disappoint.'

There is another garden of Queen Mary's, which may still be seen, and which has been left to itself like that in the Isle of Rest. It is in the grounds of Chatsworth, and is moated, walled round, and raised about fifteen feet above the park. Here the Queen, when a prisoner under the charge of 'Old Bess of Hardwick', was allowed to walk without any guard. How different the two! And how different she who took her pleasure in them!

# ALEXANDER MACKENZIE

## THE HIGHLAND CLEARANCES

· · ✳ · ·

THE Sutherland clearances were commenced in a comparatively mild way in 1807, by the ejection of ninety families from Farr and Lairg. These were provided for, some fifteen or seventeen miles distant, with smaller lots, to which they were permitted to remove their cattle and plenishing, leaving their crops un-protected, however, in the ground from which they were evicted. They had to pull down their old houses, remove the timber, and build new ones, during which period they had in many cases to sleep under the open canopy of heaven. In the autumn they carried away, with great difficulty, what remained of their crops, but the fatigue incurred cost a few of them their lives, while others contracted diseases which stuck to them during the remainder of their lives, and shortened their days.

In 1809 several hundred were evicted from the parishes of Dornoch, Rogart, Loth, Clyne, and Golspie, under circumstances of much greater severity than those already described. Several were driven by various means to leave the country altogether, and to those who could not be induced to do so, patches of moor and bog were offered on Dornoch Moor and Brora Links—quite unfit for cultivation. This process was carried on annually until, in 1811, the land from which the people were ejected was divided into large farms, and advertised as huge sheep runs. The country was overrun with strangers who came to look at these extensive tracts. Some of these gentlemen got up a cry that they were afraid of their lives among the evicted tenantry. A trumped-up story was manufactured that one of the interlopers was pursued by some of the natives of Kildonan, and put in bodily fear. The military were sent for from Fort George. The 21st Regiment was marched to Dunrobin Castle, with artillery and cartloads of ammunition. A great farce was performed; the people were sent for by the factors to the Castle at a certain hour. They came peaceably, but the farce must be gone through, the Riot Act was read; a few sheepish, innocent Highlanders were made prisoners, but nothing could be laid to their charge, and they were almost immediately set at liberty, while the soldiers were ordered back to Fort George. The demonstration, however, had the desired effect of cowing and frightening the people into the most absolute submission. They became dismayed and broken-hearted, and quietly submitted to their fate. The clergy all this time were assiduous in preaching that all the misfortunes of the people were 'fore-ordained of God, and denouncing the vengeance of Heaven and eternal damnation on all those who would presume to make the slightest resistance'. At the May term of 1812 large districts of these parishes were cleared in the most peaceable manner, the poor creatures foolishly believing the false teaching of their selfish and dishonest spiritual guides—save the mark! The Earl of Selkirk, who went personally to the district, allured many of the evicted people to emigrate to his estates on the Red River in British North America, whither a whole ship-cargo of them went. After a long and otherwise disastrous passage they found themselves deceived and deserted by the Earl, left to their unhappy fate in an inclement wilderness, without any protection from the hordes of Red Indian savages by whom the district was infested, and who plundered them of their all on their arrival and finally massacred them, save a small remnant who managed to escape, and travelled, through immense difficulties, across trackless forests to Upper Canada.

The notorious Mr. Sellar was at this time sub-factor, and in the spring of 1814 he took a large portion of the parishes of Farr and Kildonan into his own hands. In the month of March the old tenantry received notices to quit at the ensuing May term, and a few days after the summonses were served, the greater portion of the heath pasture was, by his orders, set on fire. By this cruel proceeding the cattle belonging to the old tenantry were left without food during the spring, and it was impossible to dispose of them at a fair price, the price having fallen after the war; for Napoleon was now a prisoner in Elba, and the demand for cattle became temporarily dull and prices very much reduced. To make matters worse, fodder was unusually scarce this spring, and the poor people's cattle depended for subsistence solely on the spring grass which sprouts out among the heather, but which this year had been burnt by the factor who would himself reap the benefit when he came into possession later on.

In May the work of ejectment was again commenced, accompanied by cruelties hitherto unknown even in the Highlands. Atrocities were perpetrated which I cannot trust myself to describe in my own words. I shall give what is much more valuable—a description by an eye-witness in his own language. He says: In former removals the tenants had been allowed to carry away the timber of their old dwellings to erect houses on their new allotments, but now a more summary mode was adopted by setting fire to them. The able-bodied men were by this time away after their cattle or otherwise engaged at a distance, so that the immediate sufferers by the general house-burning that now commenced were the aged and infirm, the women and children. As the lands were now in the hands of the factor himself, and were to be occupied as sheep farms, and as the people made no resistance, they expected, at least, some indulgence in the way of permission to occupy their houses and other buildings till they could gradually remove, and meanwhile look after their growing crops. Their consternation was therefore greater, when immediately after the May term-day, a commencement was made to pull down and set fire to the houses over their heads. The old people, women and others, then began to preserve the timber which was their own; but the devastators proceeded with great celerity, demolishing all before them, and when they had overthrown all the houses in a large tract of the country, they set fire to the wreck. Timber, furniture, and every other article that could not be instantly removed was consumed by fire or otherwise utterly destroyed. The proceedings were carried on with the greatest rapidity and the most reckless cruelty. The cries of the victims, the confusion, the despair and horror painted on the countenances of the one party, and the exulting ferocity of the other, beggar all description. At these scenes Mr. Sellar was present, and apparently, as sworn by several witnesses at his subsequent trial, ordering and directing the whole. Many deaths ensued from alarm, from fatigue, and cold, the people having been instantly deprived of shelter, and left to the mercies of the elements. Some old men took to the woods and to the rocks, wandering about in a state approaching to, or of absolute, insanity; and several of them in this situation lived only a few days.

'To these scenes,' says Donald Macleod, 'I was an eye-witness, and am ready to substantiate the truth of my statements. Donald Munro, Garvott, lying in a fever, was turned out of his house and exposed to the elements. Donald Macbeath, an infirm and bed-ridden old man, had the house unroofed over him, and was in a state exposed to the wind and rain until death put a period to his sufferings. I was present at the pulling down and burning of the house of William Chisholm, Badinloskin, in which was lying his wife's mother, an old bed-ridden woman of nearly 100 years of age, none of the family being present. I informed the persons about to set fire to the house of this circumstance, and prevailed on them to wait until Mr. Sellar came. On his arrival, I told him of the poor old woman being in a condition unfit for removal, when he replied, "Damn her, she has lived too long—let her burn." Fire was immediately set to the house, and the blankets in which she was carried out were in flames before she could be got out. She was placed in a little shed, and it was with great difficulty they were prevented from firing it also. The old woman's daughter arrived while the house was on fire, and assisted the neighbours in removing her mother out of the flames and smoke, presenting a picture of horror which I shall never forget, but cannot attempt to describe. Within five days she was a corpse.'

In 1816 Sellar was charged at Inverness, before the Court of Justiciary, with culpable homicide and fire-raising in connection with these proceedings, and, considering all the circumstances, it is not at all surprising that he was 'honourably' acquitted of the grave charges made against him. Almost immediately after, however, he ceased to be factor on the Sutherland estates, and Mr. Loch came into power. Evictions were carried out from 1814 down to 1819 and 1820, pretty much of the same character as those already described, but the removal of Mr. Young, the chief factor, and Mr. Sellar from power was hailed with delight by the whole remaining population. Their very names had become a terror. Their appearance in any part of the country caused such alarm as to make women fall into fits. One woman became so terrified, that she became insane, and whenever she saw anyone she did not recognize, she invariably cried out in a state of absolute terror—'Oh! sin Sellar'—'Oh! there's Sellar.' The people, however, soon discovered that the new factors were not much better. Several leases which were current would not expire until 1819 and 1820, so that the evictions were necessarily only partial from 1814 down to that period. The people were reduced to such a state of poverty that even Mr. Loch himself, in his *Sutherland Improvements*, page 76, admits that—'Their wretchedness was so great that, after pawning everything they possessed to the fishermen on the coast, such as had no cattle were reduced to come down from the hills in hundreds for the purpose of gathering cockles on the shore. Those who lived in the more remote situations of the country were obliged to subsist upon broth made of nettles, thickened with a little oatmeal. Those who had cattle had recourse to the still more wretched expedient of bleeding them, and mixing the blood with oatmeal, which they afterwards cut into slices and fried. Those who had a little money came down and slept all night upon the beach, in order to watch the boats returning from the fishing, that they might be in time to obtain a part of what had been caught.' He, however, omitted to mention the share he and his predecessors had taken in reducing the people to such misery, and the fact that at this very time he had constables stationed at the Little Ferry to prevent the starved tenantry from collecting shellfish in the only place where they could find them.

He prevailed upon the people to sign documents consenting to remove at the next Whitsunday term, promising at the same time to make good provision for them elsewhere. In about a month after, the work of demolition and devastation again commenced, and parts of the parishes of Golspie, Rogart, Farr, and the whole of Kildonan were in a blaze. Strong parties with faggots and other combustible material were set to work; three hundred houses were given ruthlessly to the flames, and their occupants pushed out in the open air without food or shelter. Macleod, who was present, describes the horrible scene as follows:

'The consternation and confusion were extreme; little or no time was given for the removal of persons or property; the people striving to remove the sick and the helpless before the fire should reach them; next, struggling to save the most valuable of their effects. The cries of the women and the children, and roaring of the affrighted cattle, hunted at the same time by the yelling dogs of the shepherds amid the smoke and fire, altogether presented a scene that completely baffles description it required to be seen to be believed. A dense cloud of smoke enveloped the whole country by day, and even extended far out to sea; at night an awfully grand but terrific scene presented itself—all the houses in an extensive district in flames at once. I myself ascended a height about eleven o'clock in the evening, and counted two hundred and fifty blazing houses, many of the owners of which were my relations, and all of whom I personally knew, but whose present condition—whether in or out of the flames—I could not tell. The conflagration lasted six days, till the whole of the dwellings were reduced to ashes or smoking ruins. During one of these days a boat actually lost her way in the dense smoke as she approached the shore, but at night was enabled to reach a landing-place by the lurid light of the flames.'

The whole of the inhabitants of Kildonan, numbering nearly 2000 souls, except three families, were utterly rooted and burnt out, and the whole parish converted into a solitary wilderness. The suffering was intense. Some lost their reason. Over a hundred souls took passage to Caithness in a small sloop, the master humanely agreeing to take them in the hold, from which he had just unloaded a cargo of quicklime. A head storm came on, and they were nine days at sea in the most miserable condition—men, women, and helpless children huddled up together, with barely any provisions. Several died in consequence, and others became invalids for the rest of their days. One man, Donald Mackay, whose family was suffering from a severe fever, carried two of his children a distance of twenty-five miles to this vessel. Another old man took shelter in a meal mill, where he was kept from starvation by licking the meal refuse scattered among the dust on the floor, and protected from the rats and other vermin by his faithful collie. George Munro, the miller at Farr, who had six of his family down with fever, had to remove them in that state to a damp kiln, while his home was given to the flames. All this was done in the name of proprietors who could not be considered tyrants in the ordinary sense of the term.

# THE GAZETTEER OF SCOTLAND (1848)

## THE SOLWAY

. . * . .

THE Solway, as to the depth of its water, the character of its beach, and especially the phenomena of its tides, differs widely from every other firth in Scotland or even from every other marine indentation in the world. . . . Over a distance of about twenty miles from its head, the whole of its bed, excepting the narrow and canal-like channels of the Nith and the confluent waters which enter near the eastern extremity, is alternately a surgy brown sea, tinctured with silt, and oscillating with the rebound of the tide, and a naked, flat, unrelieved expanse of sand, a wilderness of desolation, a miniature Sahara, strangely interposing its dark dreary projection between the blooming slopes of Cumberland and the finely outlined and warmly tinted lands of Scotland. Much of its beach, or rather of its bed, even its broader and more seaward parts, is of the same character; so very much, indeed, that were the firth admeasured only by the space it covers at low water, it would figure in comparative insignificance or exceedingly limited proportions. All its tides are rapid and constitute rather a rush or careering race than a flow or a current of waters. A spring tide, but especially a tide which runs before a stiff breeze from the south or the south-west, careers along at the rate of from eight to ten miles an hour. It is heard by the people along the shore upwards of twenty miles before it reaches them, and approaches with a hoarse and loud roar and with a brilliance of phenomena and demonstration incomparably more sublime than if the wide sandy waste were densely scoured with the fleetest and most gorgeously appointed invading army of horsemen.

Before the wave can be descried from the shore, a long cloud or bank of spray is seen, as if whirling on an axis, and evanescently zoned and gemmed with mimic rainbows and rich tintings of partial refractions sweeping onward with the speed of a strong and steady breeze; then follows a long curved white and flowing surf: and when the magnificent banner of spray, and this surfy pioneer have made distinct announcement, finally and suddenly appears the majestic van of the tide, a speckled and deeply dimpled body of waters, from three to six feet high abreast, rolling impetuously forward, and bringing closely in its rear a tumbling mass of marine vales and hillocks, glittering and gorgeous all over with the most fitful play of the prismatic colours. As the tide enters the contracted parts of the firth and the lower parts of the side estuaries, it acquires such additional features of romance and novelty as render it altogether an object *per se*, and one of the most interesting that can form a main feature of any landscape. Accidents occasionally occur with ships, and have been very frequent, though much less so of late years than before, with persons venturing within high-water mark. The rivers which traverse the bed of the firth being easily fordable, strong inducement is offered by the shortness of the path to cross the sands to England during the recess of the tide. But Scotchmen, even when well mounted, have in numerous instances and occasionally to an amount constituting a literal catastrophe, been overtaken and drowned while returning from the Cumberland fairs. Even persons best acquainted with the locality are liable to be mistaken in their calculations of the time when the tide will approach; and when they have proceeded partly across may hear the appalling sound of the watery invasion so near and menacing, that a clear atmosphere, a good steed, much self-collectedness and a steady remembrance of the direction of the path, may all be necessary for their preservation. Dense fogs frequently arise and so bewilder professed and experienced guides, that they can proceed in safety only with the aid of the compass; and quicksands are occasionally formed, and fitfully shift their localities, obscurely but awfully menacing every intruder who has not watched the impressions made upon the ground by almost every successive tide.


# HUGH MILLER

## STRANGE CUSTOMS

· · ✳ · ·


I QUITTED the dame's school at the end of the first twelve-month, after mastering that grand acquirement of my life—the art of holding converse with books; and was transferred straightforth to the grammar school of the parish, at which there attended at this time about a hundred and twenty boys, with a class of about thirty individuals more, much looked down upon by the others, and not deemed greatly worth counting, seeing that it consisted of only lassies.

The old parish school of the place had been nobly situated in a snug corner, between the parish churchyard and a thick wood; and from the interesting centre which it formed, the boys, when tired of making dragoon-horses of the erect headstones, or of leaping along the flat-laid memorials, from end to end of the graveyard, 'without touching grass', could repair to the taller trees, and rise in the world by climbing among them. As, however, they used to encroach, on these latter occasions, upon the laird's pleasure-grounds, the school had been removed ere my time to the sea-shore; where, though there were neither tomb-stones nor trees, there were some balancing advantages, of the kind which perhaps only boys of the old school could have adequately appreciated.

As the school-windows fronted the opening of the Firth, not a vessel could enter the harbour that we did not see; and, improving through our opportunities, there was perhaps no educational institution in the kingdom in which all sorts of barques and carvels, from the fishing yawl to the frigate, could be more correctly drawn on the slate or where any defect of hull or rigging, in some faulty delineation, was surer of being more justly or unsparingly criticized. All the herring boats during the season passed our windows on their homeward way to the harbour; and, from their depth in the water, we became skilful enough to predicate the number of crans aboard of each with wonderful judgment and correctness. In days of good general fishing, too, when the curing-yards proved too small to accommodate the quantities brought ashore, the fish used to be laid in glittering heaps opposite the school-house door; and an exciting scene, that combined the bustle of the workshop with the confusion of the crowded fair, would straightway spring up with twenty yards of the forms on which we sat, greatly to our enjoyment, and of course, not a little to our instruction. We could see, simply by peering over book or slate, the curers going rousing their fish with salt, to counteract the effects of the dog-day sun; bevies of young women employed as gutters, squatting around the heaps, knife in hand, and plying with busy fingers their well-paid labours, at the rate of sixpence an hour; relays of heavily-laden fish-wives bringing ever and anon fresh heaps of herrings in their creels; and outside of all, the coopers hammering as if for life and death—now tightening hoops, and now slackening them, and anon caulking with bulrush the leaky seams.

The building in which we met was a long, low, straw-thatched cottage, open from gable to gable, with a mud floor below and an unlathed roof above; and stretching along the naked rafters, which, when the master chanced to be absent for a few minutes, gave noble exercise in climbing, there used frequently to lie a helm, or oar, or boathook, or even foresail—the spoil of some hapless peat-boat from the opposite side of the Firth. The Highland boatmen of Ross had carried on a trade in peats for ages with the Saxons of the town; and as every boat owed a long-derived perquisite of twenty peats to the grammar school, and as payment was at times foolishly refused, the party of boys commissioned by the master to exact it almost always succeeded, either by force or stratagem, in securing and bringing along with them, on behalf of the institution, some spar, or sail, or piece of rigging, which, until redeemed by special treaty, and the payment of the peats, was stowed up over the rafters.

These peat-expeditions, which were intensely popular in the school, gave noble exercise to the faculties. It was always a great matter to see, just as the school met, some observant boy appear, cap in hand, before the master, and intimate the fact of an arrival at the shore, by the simple words, 'Peat-boat, Sir'. The master would then proceed to name a party, more or less numerous, according to the exigency; but it seemed to be a matter of pretty correct calculation that, in the cases in which the peat claim was disputed, it required about twenty boys to bring home the twenty peats, or lacking these, the compensatory sail or spar.

There were certain ill-conditioned boatmen who almost always resisted, and who delighted to tell us—invariably, too, in very bad English—that our perquisite was properly the hangman's perquisite, made over to us because we were like him; not seeing—blockheads as they were!—that the very admission established in full the rectitude of our claim, and gave us, amid our dire perils and faithful contendings, the strengthening consciousness of a just quarrel. In dealing with these recusants, we used ordinarily to divide our forces into two bodies, the larger portion of the party filling their pockets with stones, and ranging themselves on some point of vantage, such as the pier head; and the smaller stealing down as near the boat as possible, and mixing themselves up with the purchasers of the peats. We then, after due warning, opened fire on the boatmen; and, when the pebbles were hopping about them like hailstones, the boys below commonly succeeded in securing, under cover of the fire, the desired boathook or oar. And such were the ordinary circumstances and details of this piece of Spartan education; of which a townsman has told me he was strongly reminded when boarding, on one occasion, under cover of a well-sustained discharge of musketry, the vessel of an enemy that had been stranded on the shores of Berbice.

Our school, like almost all the other grammar-schools of the period in Scotland, had its yearly cock-fight, preceded by two holidays and a half, during which the boys occupied themselves in collecting and bringing up their cocks. And such always was the array of fighting birds mustered on the occasion, that the day of the festival, from morning till night, used to be spent in fighting out the battle.

For weeks after it had passed, the school-floor would continue to retain its deeply-stained blotches of blood, and the boys would be full of exciting narratives regarding the glories of gallant birds, who had continued to fight until both their eyes had been picked out, or who, in the moment of victory, had dropped dead in the middle of the cock-pit.

The yearly fight was the relic of a barbarous age; and, in at least one of its provisions, there seemed evidence that it was that of an intolerant age also: every pupil at school, without exemption, had his name entered on the subscription-list, as a cock-fighter, and was obliged to pay the master at the rate of twopence per head, ostensibly for leave to bring his birds to the pit; but, amid the growing humanities of a better time, though the twopence continued to be exacted, it was no longer imperative to bring the birds; and availing myself of the liberty I never brought any. Nor, save for a few minutes, on two several occasions, did I ever attend the fight. I continued to pay my yearly sixpence, as a holder of three cocks—the lowest sum deemed in any degree genteel—but remained simply a fictitious or paper cock-fighter.

*from* MY SCHOOLS AND SCHOOLMASTERS

# SCOTLAND YESTERDAY

## FICTION

# ROBERT LOUIS STEVENSON

## BLACK ANDY'S TALE

. . \* . .

It was in the year seeventeen hunner and sax that the Bass cam into the hands o' the Da'rymples, and there was twa men sought the chairge of it. Baith were weel qualified for they had baith been sodgers in the garrison and kent the gate to handle solans, and the seasons and values of them. The first of them was Tam Dale, my faither. The second was ane Lapraik, whom the folk ca'd Tod Lapraik maistly, but whether for his name or his nature I could never tell.

Aweel, my faither got the Bass and Tod had to go wantin'. It was remembered sinsyne what way he had ta'en the thing. 'Tam,' says he, 'ye hae gotten the better o' me aince mair, and I hope,' says he, 'ye'll find a' that ye expeckit at the Bass;' which have since been thought remarkable expressions. At last the time came for Tam Dale to take the young solans. This was a business he was weel used wi'; he had been a craigsman frae a laddie, and trusted nane but himsel'. So there he was, hingin' by a line an' speldering[1] on the craig face, whaur it's hieest and steighest.[2] Fower tentie[3] lads were on the tap hauldin' the line and minding for the signals. But whaur Tam hung there was naething but the craig, and the sea below and the solans skirling and flying. It was a braw spring morn, and Tam whustled as he claught in the young geese. Mony's the time I heard him tell of this experience, and aye the sweat ran upon the man.

It chanced, ye see, that Tam keekit[4] up, and he was awaur of a

---

[1] spreading his limbs     [2] steepest     [3] careful     [4] looked

muckle solan, and the solan pyking at the line. He thought this by-ordinar[1] and outside the creature's habits. He minded that ropes was unco[2] saft things, and the solan's neb and the Bass Rock unco hard and that twa hunner feet were raither mair than he would care to fa'. 'Shoo!' says Tam. 'Awa, bird! Shoo, awa' wi' ye!' says he. The solan keekit doun into Tam's face, and there was something unco in the creature's eye.

Just the ae keek it gied, and back to the rope. But now it wroucht and warst't like a thing dementit.

There never was the solan made that wroucht as that solan wroucht; and it seemed to understand its employ brawly, birzing[3] the saft rope between the neb of it and a crunkled jag o' stane.

There gaed a cauld stend[4] o' fear into Tam's heart. 'This thing is nae bird,' thinks he. His een turnt backward in his heid and the day gaed black about him. 'If I get a dwam[5] here,' he thoucht, 'it's by wi' Tam Dale.' And he signalled for the lads to pu' him up.

And it seemed the solan knew about signals. For nae suner was the signal made than he let be the rope, spried his wings, squawked out loud, took a turn flying, and dashed straucht at Tam Dale's een. Tam had a knife, he gart[6] the cauld steel glitter. And it seemed the solan understood about knives, for nae suner did the steel glint in the sun than he gied the ae squawk, but laigher,[7] like a body disappointit, and flegged[8] aff about the roundness of the craig, and Tam saw him nae mair. And as sune as that thing was gane, Tam's heid drapt upon his shouther, and they pu'd him up like a deid corp, dadding[9] on the craig.

A dram of brandy (which he went never without) broucht him to his mind, or what was left of it. Up he sat.

'Rin, Geordie, rin to the boat, mak' sure of the boat, man—rin!' he cries, 'or yon solan'll have it awa',' says he.

| [1] unusual | [2] extremely | [3] teasing |
| [4] pang | [5] black-out | [6] made |
| [7] more faintly | [8] fluttered | [9] knocking |

The fower lads stared at ither, an' tried to whilly-wha him to be quiet. But naething would satisfy Tam Dale, till ane o' them had startit on ahead to stand sentry on the boat. The ithers askit if he was for down again.

'Na,' says he, 'and neither you nor me,' says he, 'and as sune as I can win to stand on my twa feet we'll be aff frae this craig o' Sawtan.'

Sure eneuch, nae time was lost, and that was ower muckle; for before they won to North Berwick Tam was in a crying fever. He lay a' the simmer; and wha was sae kind as come speiring[1] for him, but Tod Lapraik! Folk thocht afterwards that ilka time Tod cam near the house the fever had worsened. I kenna for that; but what I ken the best, that was the end of it.

It was about this time o' the year; my grand-faither was out at the white fishing; and like a bairn, I but to gang[2] wi' him. We had a grand take, I mind, and the way that the fish lay broucht us near in by the Bass, whaur we forgaithered wi' anither boat that belanged to a man Sandie Fletcher in Castleton. He's no lang deid, neither, or ye could speir at himsel'. Weel, Sandie hailed.

'What's yon on the Bass?' says he. 'On the Bass?' says grand-faither. 'Ay,' says Sandie, 'on the green side o't.' 'Whatten kind of a thing?' says grandfaither. 'There cannae be naething on the Bass but just the sheep.'

'It looks unco like a body,' quo' Sandie, who was nearer in. 'A body!' says we, and we nane of us likit that. For there was nae boat that could have broucht a man, and the key o' the prison yett[3] hung ower my faither's heid at hame in the press bed.

We kept the twa boats close for company, and crap in nearer hand. Grandfaither had a gless, for he had been a sailor, and the captain of a smack, and had lost her on the sands of Tay. And when we took the gless to it, sure eneuch there was a man. He

[1] asking        [2] had to go        [3] gate, door

was in a crunkle o' green brae, a wee below the chaipel, a' by
his lee-lane, and lowped and flang and danced like a daft quean[1]
at a waddin'.

'It's Tod,' says grandfaither, and passed the gless to Sandie.

'Ay, it's him,' says Sandie.

'Or ane in the likeness o' him,' says grandfaither.

'Sma' is the differ,' quo' Sandie. 'De'il or warlock, I'll try the
gun at him,' quo' he, and broucht up a fowling-piece that he
aye carried, for Sandie was a notable famous shot in all that
country.

'Haud your hand, Sandie,' says grandfaither; 'we maun see
clearer first,' says he, 'or this may be a dear day's wark to the
baith of us.'

'Hout!' says Sandie, 'this is the Lord's judgments surely!'
says he.

'Maybe ay, and maybe no,' says my grandfaither, worthy
man! 'But have you a mind of the Procurator Fiscal, that I think
ye'll have forgaithered wi' before,' says he.

This was ower true, and Sandie was a wee thing set ajee.[2]

'Aweel, Edie,' says he, 'and what would be your way of it?'

'Ou, just this,' says grandfaither. 'Let me that has the fastest
boat gang back to North Berwick, and let you bide here and
keep an eye on Thon. If I cannae find Lapraik, I'll join ye and
the twa of us'll have a crack wi' him. But if Lapraik's at hame,
I'll rin up the flag at the harbour, and ye can try Thon Thing wi'
the gun.'

Aweel, so it was agreed between them twa. I was just a bairn,
an' clum in Sandie's boat, whaur I thoucht I would see the best of
the employ. My grandsire gied Sandie a siller tester to put in his
gun wi' the loid draps, bein mair deidly again bogles. And then
the ae boat set aff for North Berwick, an' the tither lay whaur it
was and watched the wanchancy[3] thing on the brae-side.

A' the time we lay there it lowped and flang and capered and

[1] girl          [2] disconcerted          [3] unlucky

span like a tee-totum, and whiles we could hear it skelloch[1] as it span.

Weel, at the hinder end, we saw the wee flag yirk up to the mast-heid upon the harbour rocks. That was a' Sandie waited for. He up wi' the gun, took a deleeberate aim, and pu'd the trigger. There cam' a bang and then ae waefu' skirl frae the Bass. And there were we rubbin' our een and lookin' at ither like daft folk. For wi' the bang and the skirl the thing had clean disappeared. The sun glintit, the wund blew, and there was the bare yaird[2] whaur the Wonder had been lowping and flinging but ae second syne.

The hale way hame I roared and grat wi' the terror of that dispensation. The grawn folk were nane sae muckle better; there was little said in Sandie's boat but just the name of God; and when we won in by the pier, the harbour rocks were fair black wi' the folks waitin' us.

It seems they had fund Lapraik in ane of his dwams, cawing[3] the shuttle and smiling. Ae lad they sent to hoist the flag, and the rest abode there in the wabster's[4] house. You may be sure they liked it little; and looking on thon awesome thing as it cawed the shuttle. Syne, upon a suddenty, and wi' the ae dreadfu' skelloch, Tod sprang up frae his hinderlands and fell forrit on the wab, a bluidy corp.

When the corp was examined the leid draps had nae played buff upon the warlock's body; sorrow a leid drap was to be fund; but there was grandfaither's siller tester in the puddock's[5] heart of him.

*from* CATRIONA

---

[1] shout wildly  [2] earth  [3] working
[4] weaver  [5] frog's

# ALLAN CUNNINGHAM

## THE HAUNTED SHIPS

. . * . .

ONE fine harvest evening, I went aboard the shallop of Richard Faulder, of Allanbay; and, committing ourselves to the waters, we allowed a gentle wind from the east to waft us at its pleasure towards the Scottish coast. We passed the sharp promontory of Siddick; and skirting the land within a stonecast, glided along the shore till we came within sight of the ruined Abbey of Sweetheart. The green mountain of Criffel ascended beside us; and the bleat of the flocks from its summit, together with the winding of the evening horn of the reapers, came softened into something like music over land and sea.

We pushed our shallop into a deep and wooded bay, and sat silently looking on the serene beauty of the place. The moon glimmered in her rising through the tall shafts of the pines of Caerlaverock; and the sky, with scarce a cloud, showered down on wood and headland and bay the twinkling beams of a thousand stars, rendering every object visible. The tide too, was coming with that swift and silent swell observable when the wind is gentle; the woody curves along the land were filling with the flood, till it touched the green branches of the drooping trees; while in the centre current the roll and the plunge of a thousand pellocks[1] told to the experienced fisherman that salmon were abundant.

As we looked, we saw an old man emerging from a path that winded to the shore through a grove of doddered[2] hazel; he carried a halve-net on his back, while behind him came a girl,

---

[1] porpoises        [2] stunted and entangled

bearing a small harpoon with which the fishers are remarkably dexterous in striking their prey. The senior seated himself on a large grey stone which overlooked the bay, laid aside his bonnet, and submitted his bosom and neck to the refreshing sea breeze; and taking his harpoon from his attendant, sat with the gravity and composure of a spirit of the flood, with his ministering nymph behind him. We pushed our shallop to the shore, and soon stood at their side.

'This is old Mark Macmoran the mariner, with his grand-daughter Barbara,' said Richard Faulder, in a whisper that had something of fear in it; 'he knows every creek and cavern and quicksand in Solway—has seen the Spectre Hound that haunts the Isle of Man; has heard him bark, and at every bark has seen a ship sink; and he has seen, too, the Haunted Ships in full sail; and, if all tales be true, he has sailed in them himself; he's an awful person.'

Though I perceived in the communication of my friend something of the superstition of the sailor, I could not help thinking that common rumour had made a happy choice in singling out old Mark to maintain her intercourse with the invisible world. His hair, which seemed to have refused all intercourse with the comb, hung matted upon his shoulders; a kind of mantle, or rather blanket, pinned with a wooden skewer round his neck, fell mid-leg down, concealing all his nether garments as far as a pair of hose, darned with yarn of all conceivable colours, and a pair of shoes, patched and repaired till nothing of the original structure remained, and clasped on his feet with two massy silver buckles.

If the dress of the old man was rude and sordid, that of his granddaughter was gay, and even rich. She wore a bodice of fine wool, wrought round the bosom with alternate leaf and lily, and a kirtle of the same fabric; which, almost touching her white and delicate ankle, showed her snowy feet, so fairy-like and round, that they scarcely seemed to touch the grass where she stood. Her hair, a natural ornament which woman seeks much to improve, was of bright glossy brown, and encumbered rather than adorned with a snood, set thick with marine productions, among which the small clear pearl of the Solway was conspicuous.

Nature had not trusted to a handsome shape and a sylph-like air for young Barbara's influence over the heart of man; but had bestowed a pair of large bright blue eyes, swimming in liquid light, so full of love and gentleness and joy, that all the sailors from Annanwater to far Saint Bees acknowledged their power, and sang songs about the bonnie lass of Mark Macmoran. She stood holding a small gaff-hook of polished steel in her hand, and seemed not dissatisfied with the glances I bestowed on her from time to time, and which I held more than requited by a single glance of those eyes which retained so many capricious hearts in subjection.

The tide, though rapidly augmenting, had not yet filled the bay at our feet. The moon now streamed fairly over the tops of Caerlaverock pines, and showed the expanse of ocean dimpling and swelling, on which sloops and shallops came dancing, and displaying at every turn their extent of white sail against the beam of the moon. I looked on old Mark the mariner, who, seated motionless on his grey stone, kept his eye fixed on the increasing waters with a look of seriousness and sorrow in which I saw little of the calculating spirit of a mere fisherman. Though he looked on the coming tide, his eyes seemed to dwell particularly on the black and decayed hulls of two vessels, which, half immersed in the quicksand, still addressed to every heart a tale of shipwreck and desolation. The tide wheeled and foamed around them; and, creeping inch by inch up the side, at last fairly threw its waters over the top, and a long and hollow eddy showed the resistance which the liquid element received.

The moment they were fairly buried in the water, the old man clasped his hands together, and said:

'Blessed be the tide that will break over ye and bury ye for ever! Sad to mariners and sorrowful to maids and mothers, has the time been you have choked up this deep and bonnie bay. For evil were you sent, and for evil you have continued. Every season finds from you its song of sorrow and wail, its funeral processions, and its corpses. Woe to the land where the wood grew that made ye! Cursed be the axe that hewed ye on the mountains, the hands that joined ye together, the bay ye first swam in, and the wind that wafted ye here! Seven times have ye put my life in peril, three fair sons have ye swept from my side, and two bonnie grand-bairns; and now, even now, your waters foam and flash for my destruction, did I venture my infirm limbs in quest of food in your deadly bay. I see by that ripple and that foam, and hear by the sound and singing of your surge, that ye yearn for another victim; but it shall not be me nor mine. . . . '

Turning to my friend and me, the old man continued, 'Of the time and cause of their destruction, I know nothing certain: they have stood as you have seen them for uncounted time; and while all other ships wrecked on this unhappy coast have gone to pieces, and rotted and sunk away in a few years, these two haunted hulks have neither sunk in the quicksand, nor has a single spar on board been displaced. Maritime legend says, that two ships of Denmark having had permission, for a time, to work deeds of darkness and dolour on the deep, were at last condemned to a whirlpool and the sunken rock, and were wrecked in this bonnie bay, as a sign to seamen to be gentle and devout. The night when they were lost was a harvest evening of uncommon mildness and beauty: the sun had newly set; the moon came brighter and brighter out; and the reapers, laying their sickles at the root of the standing corn, stood looking at the increasing magnitude of the waters, for the sea and land were visible from Saint Bees to Barnhourie.

'The sails of two vessels were soon seen bent for the Scottish coast, and, with a speed outrunning the swiftest ship, they approached the dangerous quicksands and headland of Borran-point. On the deck of the foremost ship not a living soul was seen, or shape, unless something in darkness and form resembling a human shadow could be called a shape, which flitted from extremity to extremity of the ship, with the appearance of trimming the sails, and directing the vessel's course.

But the decks of its companion were crowded with human shapes; the captain and mate, the sailor and cabin-boy, all seemed there; and from them the sound of mirth and minstrelsy echoed over land and water. The coast which they skirted along was one of extreme danger, and the reapers shouted to warn them to beware of sandbank and rock; but of this friendly counsel no notice was taken, except that a large and famished dog, which sat on the prow, answered every shout with a loud, long, and melancholy howl. The deep sandbank of Carsethorn was expected to arrest the career of these desperate navigators; but they passed, with the celerity of water-fowl, over an obstruction which had wrecked many pretty ships.

'Old men shook their heads and departed, saying, "We have seen the fiend sailing in a bottomless ship; let us go home and pray"; but one young and wilful man said, "Fiend! I'll warrant it's nae fiend, but douce Janet Withershins the witch, holding a carouse with some of her Cumberland cummers,[1] and mickle red wine will be spilt atween them. Dod, I would gladly have a toothfu'! I'll warrant it's nane o' your cauld, sour slae-water like a bottle of Bailie Skrinkie's port, but right drap-o'-my-heart's-blood stuff, that would waken a body out of their last linen. I wonder where the cummers will anchor their craft?" "And I'll vow," said another rustic, "the wine they quaff is none of your visionary drink, such as a drouthie[2] body has dished out to his lips in a dream; nor is it shadowy and un-substantial, like the vessels they sail in, which are made out of a cockel-shell or a cast-off slipper, or the paring of a seaman's

---

[1] gossips        [2] thirsty, dry

right thumb-nail. I once got a hansel[1] out of a witch's quaigh[2] myself—auld Marion Mathers, of Dustiefoot, whom they tried to bury in the old kirkyard of Dunscore; but the cummer raise as fast as they laid her down, and naewhere else would she lie but in the bonnie green kirkyard of Kier, among douce[3] and sponsible fowk. So I'll vow that the wine of a witch's cup is as fell liquor as ever did a kindly turn to a poor man's heart; and be they fiends, or be they witches, if they have red wine asteer, I'll risk an drouket[4] sark[5] for ae glorious tout on't.''

' "Silence, ye sinners," said the minister's son of a neighbouring parish, who united in his own person his father's lack of devotion with his mother's love of liquor. ''Whist!—speak as if ye had the fear of something holy before ye. Let the vessels run their own way to destruction: who can stay the eastern wind, and the current of the Solway sea? I can find ye scripture warrant for that; so let them try their strength on Blawhooly rocks, and their might on the broad quicksand. There's a surf running there would knock the ribs together of a galley built by the imps of the pit, and commanded by the Prince of Darkness. Bonnilie and bravely they sail away there, but before the blast blows by they'll be wrecked; and red wine and strong brandy will be as rife as dyke water, and we'll drink the health of bonnie Bell Blackness out of her left-foot slipper.''

'The speech of the young profligate was applauded by several of his companions, and away they flew to the bay of Blawhooly, from whence they never returned. The two vessels were observed all at once to stop in the bosom of the bay, on the spot where their hulls now appear; the mirth and minstrelsy waxed louder than ever, and the forms of maidens, with instruments of music and wine cups in their hands, thronged the decks. A boat was lowered, and the same shadowy pilot who conducted the ships made it start towards the shore with the rapidity of lightning,

---

[1] gift to bring luck  [2] shallow drinking cup  [3] respectable
[4] soaked  [5] shirt

and its head knocked against the bank where the four young men stood who longed for the unblest drink. They leaped in with a laugh, and with a laugh they were welcomed on deck; wine cups were given to each, and as they raised them to their lips the vessels melted away beneath their feet; and one loud shriek, mingled with laughter still louder, was heard over land and water for many miles. Nothing more was heard or seen till the morning, when the crowd who came to the beach saw with fear and wonder the two Haunted Ships, such as they now seem, masts and tackle gone; nor mark, nor sign, by which their name, country, or destination could be known, was left remaining. Such is the tradition of the mariners; and its truth has been attested by many whose sons and whose fathers have been drowned in the haunted bay of Blawhooly.'

# JAMES HOGG

## A STURDY BORDERER

. . \* . .

NOT very long ago, one William Laidlaw, a sturdy Borderer, went on an excursion to a remote district in the Highlands of Scotland. He was a tall and very athletic man, remarkably active, and matchless at cudgel-playing, running, wrestling, and other exercises, for which the Borderers have been noted from time immemorial. To his other accomplishments he added an excellent temper, was full of good humour, and a most capital bottle-companion.

He preferred going on foot, without any companion excepting an old oaken cudgel, which had been handed down to him from several generations, and which, by way of fancy, had been christened 'Knock-him-down'.

With his trusty friend in his hand, and fifty pounds sterling in his pocket, he found himself, by the fourth day, in one of the most dismal glens of the Highlands. It was by this time nightfall, and both William's appetite and limbs told him it was high time to look about for a place of repose, having since six in the morning walked nearly fifty English miles.

Now, the question which employed his cogitations at this moment was, whether he should proceed, at the risk of losing his way among the bogs and morasses for which this district is famed, or remain till daybreak where he was. Both expedients were unpleasant, and it is difficult to say which he would have adopted, when, about a mile to the left, a glimmering among the darkness attracted his notice.

It might have been a 'Will-o'-wisp', or the light of some evil spirit at its midnight orgies; but whatever the cause might be, it decided Mr. Laidlaw as to his further operations. He did not reflect a moment upon the matter, but exercising 'Knock-him-down' in its usual capacity of walking assistant, he found himself in a few minutes alongside the spot from which the light proceeded. It was a Highland cottage, built after the usual fashion, partly of stone and partly of turf; but without examining too minutely the exterior of the building, he applied the stick to the door with such a degree of force as he conceived necessary to arouse the inmates.

'Wha's there?' cried a shrill voice, like that of an old woman; 'what want ye at this hour of the night?'

'I want lodging, honest woman, if such a thing is to be got.'

'Na, na,' replied the inmate, 'you can get nae lodging here. Neither gentle or simple shall enter my house this night. Gang on your ways. You're no aboon five miles frae the clachan of Ballacher.'

'Five deevils!' exclaimed the Borderer; 'I tell you I have walked fifty miles already, and could as soon find out Johnny Groat's as the clachan.'

'Walk fifty more, then,' cried the obstinate portress; 'but here you downa[1] enter, while I keep you out.'

'If you come to that, my woman,' said William, 'we shall soon settle the point. In plain language, if you do not let me in wi' your gude-will I shall enter without it,' and with that he laid his shoulder to the door, with the full intention of storming the fortress. A whispering within made him pause a moment.

'And must I let him in?' murmured the old woman to someone who seemed in the interior.

'Yes,' answered the half-suppressed voice; 'he may enter—he is but one, and we are three—a lowland tup, I suppose.'

The door was slowly opened. The person who performed this unwilling act was a woman apparently about seventy, haggard and bent by an accumulation of infirmity and years. Her face was pale, malignant and wrinkled, and her little sharp peering eyes seemed, like those of the adder, to shoot forth evil upon whomsoever they gazed. As William entered, he encountered this aged sibyl, her natural hideousness exposed full to his gaze by the little rush-light she held above her head, the better to view the tall Borderer.

'You want a night's lodging, say you? Ay, nae doubt, like many others frae the south, come to trouble honest folks.'

'There's nae need to talk about troubling,' said Laidlaw. 'If you have trouble you shall be paid for it; and since you are pleased, my auld lady, to talk about the south, let me say a word of the north. I have got money in my pouch to pay my way wherever I go, and this is mair than some of your bonny Highland lairds can say. Here it lies, my lady!' and he struck with the palm of his hand the large and well-replenished pocket-book which bulged out from his side

'I want nane of your money,' said the old crone, her eyes nevertheless sparkling with malicious joy; 'walk in; you will have the company of strangers for the night.'

[1] dare not

He followed her advice, and went to the end of the cottage, near which, upon the floor, blazed a large fire of peat. There was no grate, and for a chimney a hole in the roof sufficed, through which the smoke ascended in large volumes. Here he saw the company mentioned by the sibyl. It consisted of three men, of the most fierce and savage aspect. Two of them were dressed as sailors, the third in a sort of Highland garb.

He had never seen any persons who had so completely the air of desperadoes. The first two were dark in their complexions, their black bushy beards apparently unshorn for many weeks. Their expressions were dark and ominous, and bespoke spirits within which had been trained up in crime. Nor were the red locks of the third, and his fiery countenance, and sharp cruel eyes, less appalling, and less indicative of evil.

These three men were seated around the fire; and when our traveller came alongside of them, and saluted them, not one returned his salutation. Each sat in dogged silence. If they deigned to recognize him, it was by looks of ferocious sternness, and these looks were momentary, for they instantly relapsed into their former state of sullen apathy.

William was at this time beset by two most unfortunate inclinations. He had an incorrigible desire, first, to speak, and secondly, to eat; and never had any propensities come upon a man so malapropos. He sat for a few minutes absolutely nonplussed about the method of gratifying them. At length, after revolving the matter deeply in his mind, he contrived to get out with the following words:

'I have been thinking, gudewife, that something to eat is very agreeable when a body is hungry.' No answer.

'I have been thinking, mistress, that when a man is hungry he is the better of something to eat.' No answer.

'Did you hear what I was saying, mistress?'

'Perfectly weel.'

'And what is your opinion of the matter?'

'My opinion is, that a hungry man is the better of being fed.'
Such was the old dame's reply; and he thought he could perceive
a smile of bitter ridicule curl up the savage lips of his three
neighbours.

'Was there ever such an auld hag?' thought the yeoman to
himself. 'There she sits at her wheel, and cares nae mair for a
fellow-creature than I would for a dead sheep.'

'Mistress,' continued he, 'I see you will not tak' hints. I
maun then tell you plainly that I am the next door to starvation,
and that I will thank you for something to eat.'

This produced the desired effect, for she instantly got up from
her wheel, went to a cupboard, and produced a plentiful supply
of cold venison, bread and cheese, together with a large bottle
full of the finest whisky.

William now felt quite at his ease. Putting 'Knock-him-down'
beside him, and planting himself at the table, he commenced
operations in a style that would have done honour to Friar Tuck
himself. Venison, bread, and cheese disappeared like magic. So
intently did he keep to his occupation that he neither thought
nor cared about any other object.

Everything which came under the denomination of eatable
having disappeared from the table, he proceeded to discuss the
contents of the black bottle which stood by. He probably
indulged rather freely in this respect, for shortly after commencing
he became very talkative, and seemed resolved, at all risks, to
extract conversation from his mute companions.

'You will be in the smuggling trade, frien'?' said he, slapping
the shoulder of one of his dark-complexioned neighbours. The
fellow started from his seat, and looked upon the Borderer with
an expression of anger and menace, but he was suddenly
quieted by one of his companions, who whispered into his ear,
'Hush, Roderick; never mind him; the time is not yet come.'

'I was saying, frien',' reiterated Laidlaw, without perceiving
this interruption, 'that you will be in the smuggling trade?'

'Maybe I am,' was the fellow's answer.

'And you are a fish of the same water?' continued William to the second, who nodded assent.

'And you, frien' wi' the red hair, what are ye?'

'Humph!'

'Humph!' cried the Borderer; 'that is one way of answering questions—humph, ay humph, very good; ha, ha, your health, Mr. Humph!' and he straightway swallowed another glass of the potent spirit.

These three personages, during the whole of his various harangues, preserved the same unchanged silence, replying to his broken and unconnected questions by nods and monosyllables. They even held no verbal communication with one another, but each continued apparently within himself the thread of his own gloomy meditations.

The night by this time waxed late; the spirit began to riot a little in the Borderer's head; and concluding that there was no sociality among persons who could neither drink nor speak, he quaffed off a final glass, and dropped back on his chair.

How long he remained in this state cannot be known. Certain it is, he was rather suddenly awakened from it by a hand working its way cautiously and gently into his bosom. At first he did not know what to make of this: his ideas were as yet unrallied, and by a sort of instinct he merely pressed his left hand against the spot by way of resistance. The same force continuing, however, to operate as formerly, he opened his eyes, and saw himself surrounded by the three strangers. The red-haired ruffian was the person who had aroused him—the two others, one of them armed with a cutlass, stood by. William was so astonished at this scene that he could form no opinion on the subject. His brain still rang with the strange visions that had crossed it, and with the influence of the intoxication.

'I am thinking, honest man, that you are stealing my pocket-book,' was the first ejaculation he got out with, gazing at the same time with a bewildered look on the plunderer.

'Down with the villain!' thundered one of these worthies at the same instant; 'and you sir,' brandishing the cutlass over the Borderer's head, 'resist, and I will cleave you to the collar.'

This exclamation acted like magic upon Laidlaw; it seemed to sober him in an instant, and point out his perilous situation.

The trio rushed upon him, and attempted to hold him down. Now or never was the period to put his immense strength to the trial. Collecting all his energies, he bounded from their grasp, and, his herculean fist falling like a sledge-hammer upon the forehead of him who carried the cutlass, the ruffian tumbled headlong to the earth. In a moment more he stood in the centre of the cottage, whirling 'Knock-him-down' around his head in the attitude of defiance. Such was now his appearance of determined courage and strength that the two ruffians opposed to him, although powerful men, and armed with bludgeons, did not dare to advance, but recoiled several paces from their single opponent. He had escaped thus far, but his situation was still very hazardous, for the men, though baffled, kept their eyes intently fixed upon him, and seemed only to wait an opportunity when they could rush on with most advantage. Besides, the one he had floored had just got up, and with his cutlass joined the others. If they had made an attack upon him, his great skill and vigour would in all probability have brought one of them to the ground, but then he would have been assailed by the two others; and the issue of such a contest, armed as one of them was, could not but be highly dangerous.

Meanwhile the men, although none of them ventured to rush singly upon the Borderer, began to advance in a body, as if for the purpose of getting behind him.

'Now,' thought William, 'if I can but keep you quiet till I get opposite the door, I may show you a trick that will astonish you.'

So planning his scheme, he continued retreating before his assailants, and holding up his cudgel in the true scientific position till he came within a foot of the door; most fortunately it stood wide open. One step aside, and the threshold was gained— another, and it was passed.

In the twinkling of an eye, swift like a thunderbolt, fell 'Knock-him-down' upon the head of the forward opponent, and in another, out bolted William Laidlaw from the cottage.

The whole was the work of an instant. He who received the blow fell stunned and bleeding to the ground, and his companions were so confounded that they stood mute and gazing at each other for several seconds. Their resolution was soon taken, and in a mood between shame and revenge, they sallied out after the fugitive. Their speed was, however, employed in vain against the fleetest runner of the Cheviots, and they were afraid to separate, lest each might encounter singly this formidable adversary, who perhaps might have dealt with them in the same manner as Horatius did with the Curiatii of old. The pursuit continued but a short way, as the yeoman more than double distanced his pursuers in the first two minutes, and left them no chance of coming up with him.

*from* A DREAM OF DEATH

## SIR THOMAS DICK LAUDER

### THE BURNING OF ELGIN CATHEDRAL

· · * · ·

THE vesper hymn had died away through the lengthened aisles of the venerable Cathedral; every note of labour or of mirth was silenced within the town. The weary burghers were sunk in sleep, and even the members of the various holy fraternities had retired to their repose. No eye was awake, save those of a few individuals among the religious, who, having habits of more than ordinary severity of discipline, had doomed themselves to wear the hard pavement with their bare knees, and pass the hours in endless repetition of penitential prayers before the shrine of the Virgin, or the image of some favourite saint. Not even a dog was heard to stir in the streets. They were as dark, too, as they were silent; for, with exception of a feeble lamp or two, that burned in niches, before the little figures set up here and there, there was nothing to interrupt the deep obscurity that prevailed.

Suddenly the sound of a large body of horsemen was heard entering the town from the west. The dreams of the burghers were broken, and they were roused from their slumbers; the casements were opened, one after another, as the band passed along, and many a curious head was thrust out. They moved on alertly, without talking; but though they uttered no sounds, and were but dimly seen, the clank of their weapons, and the steel harness, told well enough that they were no band of vulgar, peace-loving merchants, but a troop of stirring men-at-arms; and many was the cheek that blenched, and many was the ejaculation that escaped the shuddering lips of the timid burghers, as they shrunk within their houses at the alarming conviction. They crossed and blessed themselves after the warriors had passed by, and each again sought his bed.

But the repose of the inhabitants was for that night doomed to be short. Distant shrieks of despair, mingled with shouts of exultation, began to arise in the neighbourhood of the Cathedral and the College, in which all the houses of the canons were clustered; and soon the town was alarmed from its centre to its suburbs by the confused cries of half-naked fugitives, who hurried along into the country, as if rushing from some dreadful danger.

'Fire, fire!—murder!—fire, fire!—the Wolfe of Badenoch!'

The terrible name of the fell Earl of Buchan was enough, of itself, to have spread universal panic through the town, even in the midst of broad sunshine. But darkness now magnified their fears. Every one hastened to huddle on what garments might be at hand, and to seize what things were most valuable and portable; and all, without exception—men, women, and children—hurried out into the streets, to seek immediate safety in flight. As the crowd pressed onwards, scarcely daring to look behind them, they beheld the intense darkness of the night invaded by flames that began to shoot upwards in fitful jets. The screams and the shouts rang in their ears, and they quickened their trembling speed; their voices subdued by fear, as they went, into indistinct whispers of horror. No one dared to stop; but, urging on his own steps, he dragged after him those of his feeble parents, or tottering wife, or helpless children.

Those who were most timorous halted not until they had hid themselves in the neighbouring woods; but those whose curiosity was in some degree an equipoise to their fears, stopped to look behind them whenever a view of the town could be obtained, that they might judge of, and lament over, the devastation that was going forward. Already they could see that the College, the Church of St. Giles, the Hospital of the Maison Dieu, were burning; but these were all forgotten, as they beheld the dire spectacle of the Cathedral, illuminated throughout all the rich tracery of its Gothic windows by a furious fire, that was already raging high within it. Groans and lamentations burst from their hearts, and loud curses were poured out on the impious heads of those whose fury had led them to destroy so glorious a fabric, an edifice which they had been taught to venerate from their earliest infancy, and to which they were attached by every association, divine and human, that could possibly bind the heart of man. In the midst of their wailings, the pitchy vault of heaven began to be reddened by the glare of the spreading conflagration; and the loud and triumphant shouts that now arose, unmingled with those cries of terror which had at first blended with them, too plainly told that the power of the destroyer was resistless.

*from* THE WOLFE OF BADENOCH

# SIR WALTER SCOTT

## THE PORTEOUS RIOT

. . * . .

To Captain John Porteous, the honour of his command and of
his corps seems to have been a matter of high interest and
importance. He was exceedingly incensed against Wilson for the
affront which he construed him to have put upon his soldiers, in
the effort he made for the liberation of his companion, and
expressed himself most ardently on the subject. He was no less
indignant at the report, that there was an intention to rescue
Wilson himself from the gallows, and uttered many threats and
imprecations upon that subject, which were afterwards remembered to his disadvantage. In fact, if a good deal of determination and promptitude rendered Porteous, in one respect, fit
to command guards designed to suppress popular commotion, he
seems, on the other, to have been disqualified for a charge so
delicate, by a hot and surly temper, always too ready to come to
blows and violence; a character void of principle; and a dis-
position to regard the rabble, who seldom failed to regale him
and his soldiers with some marks of their displeasure, as declared
enemies, upon whom it was natural and justifiable that he should
seek opportunities of vengeance. Being, however, the most
active and trustworthy among the captains of the City Guard, he
was the person to whom the magistrates confided the command
of the soldiers appointed to keep the peace at the time of Wilson's
execution. He was ordered to guard the gallows and scaffold,
with about eighty men, all the disposable force that could be
spared for that duty.

But the magistrates took further precautions, which affected

Porteous's pride very deeply. They requested the assistance of part of a regular infantry regiment, not to attend upon the execution, but to remain drawn up on the principal street of the city, during the time that it went forward, in order to intimidate the multitude, in case they should be disposed to be unruly, with a display of force which could not be resisted without desperation. It may sound ridiculous in our ears, considering the fallen state of this ancient civic corps, that its officer should have felt punctiliously jealous of its honour. Yet so it was. Captain Porteous resented, as an indignity, the introducing the Welsh Fusiliers within the city, and drawing them up in the street where no drums but his own were allowed to be sounded without the special command or permission of the magistrates. As he could not show his ill-humour to his patrons the magistrates, it increased his indignation and his desire to be revenged on the unfortunate criminal Wilson, and all who favoured him. These internal emotions of jealousy and rage wrought a change on the man's mien and bearing, visible to all who saw him on the fatal morning when Wilson was appointed to suffer. Porteous's ordinary appearance was rather favourable. He was about the middle size, stout, and well made, having a military air, and yet rather a gentle and mild countenance. His complexion was brown, his face somewhat fretted with the scars of the smallpox, his eyes rather languid than keen or fierce. On the present occasion, however, it seemed to those who saw him as if he were agitated by some evil demon. His step was irregular, his voice hollow and broken, his countenance pale, his eyes staring and wild, his speech imperfect and confused, and his whole appearance so disordered, that many remarked he seemed to be fey, a Scottish expression, meaning the state of those who are driven on to their impending fate by the strong impulse of some irresistible necessity.

One part of his conduct was truly diabolical, if, indeed, it has not been exaggerated by the general prejudice entertained against his memory. When Wilson, the unhappy criminal, was delivered to him by the keeper of the prison, in order that he might be conducted to the place of execution, Porteous, not satisfied with the usual precautions to prevent escape, ordered him to be manacled. This might be justifiable from the character and bodily strength of the malefactor, as well as from the apprehensions so generally entertained of an expected rescue. But the handcuffs which were produced being found too small for the wrists of a man so big-boned as Wilson, Porteous proceeded with his own hands, and by great exertion of strength, to force them till they clasped together, to the exquisite torture of the unhappy criminal. Wilson remonstrated against such barbarous usage, declaring that the pain distracted his thoughts from the subjects of meditation proper to his unhappy condition.

'It signifies little,' replied Captain Porteous; 'your pain will soon be at an end.'

'Your cruelty is great,' answered the sufferer. 'You know not how soon you yourself may have occasion to ask the mercy, which you are now refusing to a fellow-creature. May God forgive you!'

These words, long afterwards quoted and remembered, were all that passed between Porteous and his prisoner; but as they took air, and became known to the people, they greatly increased the popular compassion for Wilson, and excited a proportionate degree of indignation against Porteous; against whom, as strict, and even violent in the discharge of his unpopular office, the common people had some real, and many imaginary causes of complaint.

When the painful procession was completed, and Wilson, with the escort, had arrived at the scaffold in the Grassmarket, there appeared no sign of that attempt to rescue him which had occasioned such precautions. The multitude, in general, looked on with deeper interest than at ordinary executions; and there might be seen, on the countenances of many, a stern and indignant expression, like that with which the ancient Cameronians might be supposed to witness the execution of their brethren, who glorified the Covenant on the same occasion, and at the same spot. But there was no attempt at violence. Wilson himself seemed disposed to hasten over the space that divided time from eternity. The devotions proper and usual on such occasions were no sooner finished than he submitted to his fate, and the sentence of the law was fulfilled.

He had been suspended on the gibbet so long as to be totally deprived of life, when at once, as if occasioned by some newly-received impulse, there arose a tumult among the multitude. Many stones were thrown at Porteous and his guards; some mischief was done; and the mob continued to press forward with whoops, shrieks, howls, and exclamations. A young fellow, with a sailor's cap slouched over his face, sprang on the scaffold, and cut the rope by which the criminal was suspended. Others approached to carry off the body, either to secure for it a decent grave, or to try, perhaps, some means of resuscitation. Captain Porteous was wrought, by this appearance of insurrection against his authority, into a rage so headlong as to make him forget, that, the sentence having been fully executed, it was his duty not to engage in hostilities with the misguided multitude, but to draw off his men as fast as possible. He sprang from the scaffold, snatched a musket from one of his soldiers, commanded the party to give fire, and, as several eye-witnesses concurred in swearing, set them the example, by discharging his piece, and shooting a man dead on the spot. Several soldiers obeyed his command or followed his example; six or seven persons were slain, and a great many were hurt and wounded.

After this act of violence, the Captain proceeded to withdraw his men towards their guard-house in the High Street. The mob were not so much intimidated as incensed by what had been done. They pursued the soldiers with execrations, accompanied by volleys of stones. As they pressed on them, the rearmost

soldiers turned, and again fired with fatal aim and execution. It
is not accurately known whether Porteous commanded this
second act of violence; but, of course, the odium of the whole
transactions of the fatal day attached to him, and to him alone.
He arrived at the guard-house, dismissed his soldiers, and went
to make his report to the magistrates concerning the unfortunate
events of the day.

Apparently by this time Captain Porteous had begun to doubt
the propriety of his own conduct, and the reception he met with
from the magistrates was such as to make him still more anxious
to gloss it over. He denied that he had given orders to fire; he
denied he had fired with his own hand; he even produced the
fusee which he carried as an officer for examination; it was found
still loaded. Of three cartridges which he was seen to put in his
pouch that morning, two were still there; a white handkerchief
was thrust into the muzzle of the piece, and returned unsoiled or
blackened. To the defence founded on these circumstances it was
answered that Porteous had not used his own piece, but had
been seen to take one from a soldier. Among the many who had
been killed and wounded by the unhappy fire, there were several
of better rank; for even the humanity of such soldiers as fired over
the heads of the mere rabble around the scaffold, proved in some
instances fatal to persons who were stationed in windows, or
observed the melancholy scene from a distance. The voice of
public indignation was loud and general; and, ere men's tempers
had time to cool, the trial of Captain Porteous took place before
the High Court of Justiciary. After a long and patient hearing, the
jury had the difficult duty of balancing the positive evidence of
many persons, and those of respectability, who deposed positively
to the prisoner's commanding his soldiers to fire, and himself
firing his piece, of which some swore that they saw the smoke
and flash, and beheld a man drop at whom it was pointed, with
the negative testimony of others, who, though well stationed for
seeing what had passed, neither heard Porteous give orders to

fire nor saw him fire himself; but, on the contrary, averred that the first shot was fired by a soldier who stood close by him. A great part of his defence was also founded on the turbulence of the mob, which witnesses, according to their feelings, their predilections, and their opportunities of observation, represented differently; some describing as a formidable riot what others represented as a trifling disturbance, such as always used to take place on the like occasions, when the executioner of the law and the men commissioned to protect him in his task were generally exposed to some indignities. The verdict of the jury sufficiently shows how the evidence preponderated in their minds. It declared that John Porteous fired a gun among the people assembled at the execution; that he gave orders to his soldiers to fire, by which many persons were killed and wounded; but, at the same time, that the prisoner and his guard had been wounded and beaten by stones thrown at them by the multitude. Upon this verdict, the Lords of Justiciary passed sentence of death against Captain John Porteous, adjudging him, in the common form, to be hanged on a gibbet at the common place of execution, on Wednesday, 8th September, 1736, and all his movable property to be forfeited to the king's use, according to the Scottish law in cases of wilful murder.

*from* THE HEART OF MIDLOTHIAN

# LOOKING TO THE PAST

## FACT

# EDWIN MUIR

## MELROSE ABBEY

· · * · ·

MELROSE Abbey lies on the opposite side of the Tweed from Galashiels, at a distance of a few miles. The houses of the pleasant little town have washed up until they almost enclose the ruins. At certain intervals between the successive English invasions the church must have been a lovely edifice; it is now, after being wrecked again and again, and neglected over long periods, indescribably pathetic. The Abbey was first founded in 1136 by David I to take the place of an ancient Culdee one in Old Melrose. It lay in the direct road of the English invaders, and was despoiled again and again. Bruce restored it in 1326, but it was once more laid waste in 1385. Towards the end of the fifteenth century it was rebuilt, but the Earl of Hertford wrecked it yet again in 1544 and 1545, and after that it did not recover. The Reformers do not seem to have 'purified' it very drastically, that is, broken its images and stolen its treasures; but neglect was in the long run equally deadly, and the ruins were for a long time used as a quarry by local house-builders. These peaceful vandals, along with five centuries of changing weather, have probably done more harm to the abbey than Calvinism and invasion combined; the west front and the west end of the nave have vanished; and a great part of the edifice is now a tranquil design drawn on beautiful old sward. A slender, pointed window, still by a miracle intact, faces one as one enters; the broken shafts in the roofless south aisle are of an exquisite lightness and grace, which their mutilation only emphasizes. It is hard to say what makes Melrose Abbey so melancholy; the remains of the fine cathedral at St. Andrews awaken a far colder response. Perhaps it is a sense of the number of times that Melrose Abbey has been destroyed; perhaps it is the great window rising beyond the line of splintered shafts as one enters. At any rate, one cannot look at it still without a feeling that with it something of transcendent loveliness passed from the life of Scotland, and something which was quite real to the people who came there once. That, whatever it was, was greater than any memorial that has survived of the life of the Borders; greater even than the Ballads.

*from* SCOTTISH JOURNEY

## AGNES MURE MACKENZIE

### THE BATTLE OF FALKIRK

· · * · ·

IT was near sunrise, and they had made seven miles of the road to Falkirk when they came on to the Scots, a great force drawn up openly on the slope of a moor. Selby's neighbour, looking under the edge of a hand, cried cheerfully, 'St. George, they're waiting for us! And dismounted, too!' Dismounted they certainly were, and arranged in a strange close formation of great circles, that seemed to have overhead a queer glittering haze. There were lesser masses, linking the circles together, and to the rearward, of all most odd positions, a small, a pitiful, body of cavalry.

The huge English column rippled to a halt. Mounted men galloped up and down the flanks, and slowly it deployed, swinging right and left until it was in the orthodox three 'battles'. Norfolk, Earl Marshal of England, commanded the right; the Church Militant, in the person of Bishop Bek, had the left, and the scarlet and gold of the royal banner showed Edward's place in the midst of the splendid ranks. Selby, watching from his station in the rear, glowed as the many pennons took the wind—score on score of them, the whole chivalry of England. Yet the ranked Scots in those queer circled formations showed no sign of moving. Someone remarked that they looked like a human castle. It was oddly true. The advance made it possible to see more clearly, and the odd glinting haze that hung above them resolved itself into spears, of fantastic length, twice at least that common, three times a man's height, ranked upright and regular like a close paling. The men between the circles were archers, though: he could see them already stringing their four-foot bows.

As the great English lines moved slowly forward, he began to make out the banners of the Scots. That heading the cavalry had three devices of some kind, gold on blue: he thought they were probably the Comyn gerbs, but with something above that might be a cadency mark. Young Comyn, then, the man they called Red John, Baliol's nephew and heir. But why was he in the rear? Surely that blue and silver flag in front must be Wallace's lion, beside the royal red one and the blue and silver again of the Scottish flag. His neighbour was growling about damned insolence. Selby's mind went back to the beam of new wood at Lanark. It was not what one wanted to think of just before action, and he hastily swung his thoughts back to the present.

The trumpets were blowing to a halt. The great rolling mass checked and hung poised, just barely out of arrow-shot from the Scots, with open grassy country between the armies. Trumpets again, and the rolling heavy thunder of the charge: the right wing had gone in, their shouts crying on St. George. The left was advancing too, the short square Bishop cantering in front. The air glinted as the Scots arrows began to fly. Not much use against men in full mail on barded horses. No stopping-power. The Scots would crumple like a handkerchief when the shock

of that heavy mass should crash against them. Even uphill it was
not too steep to gallop at the finish, and the lances were swaying
down now for the impact.

. . . But the front line were heaving and breaking into disorder. They were checked, and yet they had not reached the
Scots. If Bek. . . . No, Bek's trumpets, with a desperate note,
were blowing a halt. The Bishop had wheeled his horse, and his
arm waved over his head in urgent command. But Norfolk's
ranks were now in a milling confusion, and men were going
down, and horses: there must be a bog. He could hear, but not
make out, the shouted orders. Was Norfolk falling back? Yes,
by God, he was, and in a mess, too. Bek's wing had kept its
ranks.

Selby stood in his stirrups. The Scots had never moved. There
were gallopers riding out from the King's staff, and harsh
trumpet calls. The centre was moving now. Selby jogged his
horse. But they were not charging: they were moving to a
flank, following Bek. What the devil kind of a battle was Edward
fighting? Did he mean to stare at the Scots with two-thirds of his
force while Norfolk's men heaved and floundered in that damn
bog? Norfolk was getting them clear now, but in disorder.
Re-form out of arrow-shot, and charge again, avoiding the bog?
Yes, that would be more like it. These Scots could never stand
against mounted knights, and that handful of cavalry under the
Comyn banner would disappear like a stone in a pool of water if
they should try to do anything of the sort.

Single horsemen were shuttling back and forth with orders.
Ah, now Norfolk's men were re-forming, and quickly too. A
double charge, and the centre in to finish. The classic manœuvre.
He watched. Then the trumpets pealed, and from both flanks,
clear now of the unlucky bog, the solid masses of cavalry thundered forward, each at a slant, to strike side by side on the
unmoving Scots.

There was a curious sudden flicker in these. Shading his eyes, he saw those fantastic spears swing down, the men of the front rank dropping to their knees to make room for the spears from behind to pass over them. He barely saw it when they were blotted out by the climax and impact of the English charge. He heard the shock and the high frenzied yelling. Finis, the Scots! Yes, sure enough, their cavalry were in flight, some of Bek's flank men riding off in pursuit.

Yet the horsemen did not seem to be advancing to sweep away the main body of the Scots. Their ranks were jammed. They were eddying in confusion. Standing again in his stirrups, frozen with horror, Selby could see and grasp now what had happened. Those eighteen-foot spears, close ranked with their butts on the ground, made a wall of spikes. No reaching the men behind it till it was down. No getting through it with the ten-foot lance. No breaking it with a sword: a spear or two cut left not enough space to get through. The recoiling English ranks were leaving now a litter of writhing and struggling men and horses along the Scottish front, that walled it further. The desperate yelling rose to a madness now. What the hell—? The trumpets were blowing a retreat, and the heavy disorganized mass of cavalry falling suddenly back, pursued by Scottish arrows, but not by many, for the archers between the masses of Scottish spearmen had suffered rather severely in the charge.

The single riders were shuttling now again, the trumpets blowing. Both Bek and Norfolk—he could make out the surcoats —were hard at it, getting their men off and re-forming. But what on earth was happening in the rear?

Out of the dust came a heavy tramp of foot. Selby stared, astonished. Like almost all knights of his time he took for granted that foot were no sort of use in a pitched battle, at any rate till the opposite ranks were broken. And now Edward was bringing them up. Was the old man mad? If those Scots could break fully mailed men on barbed horses, what could . . . ? He clapped a sudden hand on his knee. That new Welsh bow they had talked so much about. He had always wanted to see it used in action.

He saw it now. The Irish and English archers were deploying, their Welsh masters, a shaggy crowd, behind and between. Why, those long bow-staves were taller than themselves, a good six feet: and the arrows—St. Peter, they must be a yard! They were stringing the bows now, a foot against the butt while the string slipped home. A few flying glints came from the Scottish lines. What was left of their archers had formed, and were shooting again, but the shafts pitched in dead ground between the armies. Now: they would advance, he supposed. Selby looked around him. Most of his neighbours still had their visors raised. The younger men watched with fascinated eyes. The older were grinning: they had fought in Edward's Welsh war, and faced the long-bow, but had never seen it used in mass like this.

Selby stared, his mouth open. The whole thing was leisurely. The men shuffled into rank to the shouting of orders. The great bows swung, the steel arrow-heads glinted as the men nocked and drew, and a thin level cloud seemed to flash against the Scots. With incredible quickness another followed it: the air hummed with the twang of strings and the whine of arrows. The beautiful rhythmic movement held Selby's eye, till triumphant cheering made him look back at the Scots. The human castle was wavering at last. No sign of flight, but the tall spears were sinking and crossing: the points rippled as men closed up the space of the dead or dragged in the wounded.

Again and again came the singing twang and whine: then more shouting halted it. It came again, but the tune was different now. They were not shooting at the whole mass of the Scots, but concentrating on points here and there. The steady ranks were showing spaces now as the gaps grew too large to fill in over the dead. Trumpets now—trumpets. It was the charge at last. Selby dragged down his visor with his bridle-hand, dropped his lance to the rest and settled well home in stirrups and high croupe as the whole English line thundered forward at the gallop against the breached schiltroms of the Scottish foot.

*from* APPRENTICE MAJESTY

## SETON GORDON

### THE MASSACRE OF GLENCOE

. . * . .

No fitter glen than Glencoe for a dark deed could be imagined. The great hills which rise from it hide the summer sun. Highest of them all is Bidean nam Beann, 3766 feet above the sea and the highest hill of Argyll. Near it stand Beinn Fhada (the Long Hill), 3500 feet, and Stob Coire an Lochain, while at the head of the glen Buchaille Etive Mór, the Great Herdsman of Etive, rises in majesty to a height of 3345 feet above the Atlantic.

The headwaters of the River Cona or Coe are incomparatively open country, and the stream enters the glen through a dark gorge, a place of gloomy waterfalls where the uruisks and other goblins may have sported in the old days, before the speedway which has been driven through the glen caused them to shun the place. The river hurries through the glen where, set high on the rocky slope of Aonach Dubh, is to be seen Ossian's Cave, inaccessible to all except skilled climbers. The Fèinne or Fingalians are elsewhere commemorated in the district, for the hill which rises to the east of the river near the foot of the glen is named Sgùrr na Fèinne—the Peak of the Fingalians. Ossian or Oisein was a leading member of the Fèinne.

There are many side glens throughout the length of Glencoe; they wind deep into the hills and are soon lost to view. The side glen that is chief in size, and also chief in interest, is Gleann

Leac na Muidhe. This grassy glen, now almost unpopulated, had many living families in it during the early seventeenth century up to the night of the massacre. So intensively was the ground cultivated that on the steep slopes low walls of turf and stone were built in order to retain the soil, which would otherwise have been washed away by the rainstorms of autumn and winter— for Glencoe is one of the wettest districts of the West Highlands, with a rainfall of over a hundred inches in the year. . . .

\*    \*    \*    \*    \*    \*

The mind must go back long years to that winter day in February, 1692, when the snow which lay deep in the glen was reddened by the blood of those massacred. Trouble had been brewing for some time. MacDonald of Glencoe, he who in the Highlands was always known as MacIain, had incurred the enmity of the Campbells, and both Argyll and Breadalbane would have liked to have seen him and his small clan out of their way. The opportunity arose sooner than could have been expected. The Highland chiefs had been required to swear allegiance to King William's Government before the first day of January, 1692. Glengarry, Lochiel, and MacIain put off the swearing until the last possible moment. The two former chiefs had the support of powerful clans; besides, they may have just succeeded in making their submission before the close of the period of grace.

At the last minute MacIain of Glencoe rode through a storm of snow to Fort William, reaching the commandant's quarters at the Garrison (as Fort William was then called) at night. Colonel Hill received MacIain in a friendly manner, but told him that he had no power to swear him (which was true enough) and that he must ride at once to Inveraray to swear before Sir Colin Campbell of Ardkinglas, the sheriff. He had two days to cover the district—and he arrived too late. Too late by a single day.

His misfortunes did not end there, for Sir Colin was from home. Impatiently MacIain awaited his return, and when he did arrive three days afterwards he told the chieftain that he could do nothing for him, since the period of grace had expired. MacIain would not take his refusal, and represented to the sheriff that it was only because the heavy snow had made the journey hazardous that he was late. So in the end Sir Colin Campbell relented and agreed to swear him, although he was unable to say that the submission would be accepted by the Government. This was on January 6, 1692.

MacIain returned home and was at home when, at the end of January, a party of 120 men of the Earl of Argyll's regiment under the command of Captain Campbell of Glenlyon were seen marching through the glen. When he saw Glenlyon, MacIain no doubt recalled uneasily that his men had 'lifted' the cattle from Glenlyon on their way home after the Battle of Killiecrankie, and his welcome of the strangers cannot have been too enthusiastic. When it was seen who they were, his eldest son at the head of twenty men went forward to meet the Campbells and asked the reason of their visit. Glenlyon and his officers gave their 'parole of honour' that they had come as friends, and asked that they might find quarters in the glen, giving as their reason the 'thronged' state of the garrison quarters at Fort William. A younger son of MacIain was married to Glenlyon's niece, and this may have influenced the people of Glencoe in accepting the assurances of goodwill, plausibly given.

For a fortnight the military remained in Glencoe and during that time mistrust gradually gave place to goodwill. Captain Campbell then received a fateful letter from Major Robert Duncanson. The letter is still in existence, and is in the Scottish National Library in Edinburgh. In it Captain Campbell is ordered to 'fall upon the MacDonalds of Glenco, and to putt all to the sword under seventy'. He is further ordered to 'have a special care that the old fox and his sones doe not escape'.

Captain Campbell of Glenlyon and his men were quartered up and down Glencoe. Canon MacInnes, who had lived in

Glencoe for more than seventy years and was a man of much lore, told me that the firm tradition of the glen was that MacIain was not living at the time of the massacre at his house at Invercoe (as most accounts of the affair have stated), but at his sheep farm in Gleann Leac na Muidhe (incorrectly named by John Buchan in his *Massacre of Glencoe* as Gleann Leac-nam-Bhuidhe). Captain Campbell of Glenlyon, if we credit a letter written on April 20 of the year of the massacre, had the evening before played at cards with MacIain, who was entirely unsuspecting, until supper. The parting between the two had been friendly, and Glenlyon had accepted an invitation to dinner on the following day.

Although the orders for the massacre had been kept secret, some news of it had leaked out. A soldier quartered on two brothers asked his hosts to take an evening walk with him. When they reached a large stone in the field the soldier thus addressed it, 'Grey stone, if I were you, I would be moving from here, for great things will happen tonight.' One of the brothers realized that he was being warned; he did not return home and escaped with his life, but his brother did return home, and was killed. On the night before the massacre MacIain's elder son, Alexander, having his suspicions, left the house. He saw a party of soldiers in the snow, was able to approach them unseen, and overheard a conversation. One soldier was saying there were things which even a common soldier could not be expected to do; that he was ready to fight the men of the glen, but not to murder them. His companion replied that duty was duty, however unpleasant it might be. Alexander at once returned to his father's house, told him what he had overheard, and urged him to leave. The old man could not bring himself to believe that things were as his son said, but agreed that he ought to continue his watch. It was some hours later that the suspicions of Alexander were confirmed. He then endeavoured to warn his father, but found the house closely surrounded by troops, and was unable to pass through the cordon. At five o'clock in the morning, in the cold, grim hour before the winter dawn, he heard the report of a gun or small cannon. It was the signal for the massacre to begin.

Loud knocks on his door caused MacIain to start from his bed and to hurry to open it. As a welcome he received a mortal wound from a gun fired at point-blank range. 'He fell,' as we read in a contemporary account, 'back into the arms of his lady, who uttered a dreadful shriek. She was stripped naked, ruffians pulled the rings from her fingers with their teeth, and she received such treatment that she died the following day.' Meanwhile men and boys were being slain without mercy. There is a story that a woman escaped with her child and hid in the bed of a precipitous burn. An officer saw them, and sent a soldier to kill the pair. The man disliked his orders so much that he killed a dog and, returning, showed his officer the animal's blood on his sword as a proof that he had carried out his orders. Thirty-eight men, women, and children were murdered that February morning; many more perished in the flight across the hill passes, 'wrestling with a storm' as a contemporary account has it. At the head of the glen was Colonel Hamilton with 400 men. His orders had been to march down the glen before daylight and cut off those endeavouring to escape to the south. He arrived late, being impeded, as he said, by the extreme severity of the weather, and his tardy arrival undoubtedly saved many lives. He is indeed credited with having slain an old man of over eighty years, the sole survivor of the people of the glen. It is said that Maclain's grandson, with his nurse, was for some years after the massacre sheltered in secret by the Campbells of Dunstaffnage, who were related by marriage to the MacDonalds. The houses of the unfortunate people were fired, and a letter of the time records that 900 cows, 200 horses, and many sheep and goats were driven from the glen.

The men of Glencoe, taken thus by surprise, what chance had they of defending themselves? Very little, yet it is known that they accounted for at least three members of Argyll's regiment.

The grave of one soldier is beneath a very old hawthorn bush which, it is said in the glen, was an old tree even at the time of the massacre. The two other soldiers were buried at a place named Cladh nan Guibhneach, near the old road. The word 'Guibhneach' is dialectal for Duibneach, and means a member of the Clan Campbell, so that eminent Celtic scholar, Professor W. J. Watson, told me. Glencoe is still a desolate glen; it has never recovered from that night's work of long ago. The side glen where MacIain was living—Gleann Leac na Muidhe—still shows the ruins of small dwellings, but there is now only one house in that glen. Scarcely visible are the ruins of MacIain's house, for water from the hills has brought down much debris during the centuries and a part of the ruined walls is now buried. A bagpipe chanter was not so long ago unearthed here; it may have been silent since the evening before the massacre, when a sacred Highland tradition was violated and the honour of those in high places deeply involved.

The croak of the raven and, more rarely, the shrill yelp of the eagle break the great silence in Glencoe. Sometimes, in spring, the roar of an avalanche from the high ridges of Bidean nam Beann sounds like prolonged thunder, so that the deer seek safety in flight and the ptarmigan rise, white-winged, into the heavens. The winds often rush through the glen, and lift the water from the swaying cascades so that, defying the law of gravity, it disappears into the clouds that are tempest-torn as they race over the jagged peaks. But when you have emerged from the glen, and have reached King's House, you find here an open country, still wet and stormy it is true, but giving wide views and receiving the benefit of any sunshine there may be.

*from* THE HIGHLANDS OF SCOTLAND

---

## LOOKING TO THE PAST

### FICTION

# JOHN BUCHAN

## THE SPATE IN TWEED

· · \* · ·

THE year 1683 was with us the driest year in any man's history. From the end of April to the end of July we had scarce a shower. The hay harvest was ruined beyond repair, and man and beast were sick with the sultry days. It was on the last Monday of July that I, wearied with wandering listlessly about the house, bethought myself of riding to Peebles to see the great match at bowls which is played every year for the silver horn. I had no expectation of a keen game, for the green was sure to be well-nigh ruined with the sun, and men had lost spirit in such weather. But the faintest interest is better than purposeless idleness, so I roused myself from languor and set out.

I saddled Maisie the younger, for this is a family name among our horses, and rode down by the Tweed side to the town. The river ran in the midst of a great bed of sun-baked gravel—a little trickle that a man might step across. I do not know where the fish had gone, but they, too, seemed scared by the heat, for not a trout plashed to relieve the hot silence. When I came to the Manor pool I stood still in wonder, for there for the first time in my life I saw the stream dry. Manor, which is in winter a roaring torrent, and at other times a clear, full stream, had not a drop of running water in its bed: naught but a few stagnant pools green with slime. It was a grateful change to escape from the sun into the coolness of the Neidpath woods; but even there a change was seen, for the ferns hung their fronds wearily and the moss had lost all its greenness. When once more I came out to the sun, its beating on my face was so fierce that it almost burned, and I was glad when I came to the town and the shade of tree and dwelling.

The bowling green of Peebles, which is one of the best in the country, lies at the west end of the High Street at the back of the Castle Hill. It looks down on Tweed and Peebles Water, where they meet at the Cuddie's Pool, and thence over a wide stretch of landscape to the high hills. The turf had been kept with constant waterings, but notwithstanding, it looked grey and withered. Here I found half of the men-folk of Peebles assembled, and many from the villages near, to see the match which is the greatest event of the month. Each player wore a riband of a special colour. Most of them had stripped off their coats and jerkins to give their arms free play, and some of the best were busied in taking counsel with their friends as to the lie of the green. The landlord of the Cross Keys was there with a great red favour stuck in his hat, looking, as I thought, too fat and rubicund a man to have a steady eye. Near him was Peter Crustcrackit, the tailor, a little wiry man with legs bent from sitting cross-legged, thin active hands, and keen eyes well used to the sewing of fine work. Then there were carters and shepherds, stout fellows with bronzed faces and great brawny chests, and the miller of the Wauk-mill, who was reported the best bowl player in the town. Some of the folk had come down like myself merely to watch; and among them I saw Andrew Greenlees, the surgeon, who had tended me what time I went over the cauld. A motley crowd of the odds and ends of the place hung around or sat on the low wall—poachers and black-fishers and all the riff-raff of the town.

The jack was set, the order of the game arranged, and the play commenced. A long man from the Quair Water began, and sent his bowl curling up the green not four inches from the mark.

'Weel dune for Quair Water,' said one. 'They're nane sae blind thereaways.' Then a flesher's lad came out and sent a shot close on the heels of the other and lay by his side.

At this, there were loud cries of 'Weel dune, Coo's Blether,' which was a name they had for him; and the fellow grew red and withdrew to the back.

Next came a little nervous man, who looked entreatingly at the bystanders as if to bespeak their consideration. 'Jock Look-up, my dear,' said a man solemnly, 'compose your anxious mind, for thae auld wizened airms o' yours'll no send it half-road.' The little man sighed and played his bowl; it was even as the other had said and was adjudged a hogg and put off the green.

Then many others played till the green was crowded at one end with balls. They played in rinks, and interest fell off for some little time till it came to the turn of the two acknowledged champions, Master Crustcrackit and the miller, to play against one another. Then the onlookers crowded round once more.

The miller sent a long swinging shot which touched the jack and carried it some inches onward. Then a bowl from the tailor curled round and lay between them and the former mark. Now arose a great dispute (for the players of Peebles had a way of their own, and to understand their rules required no ordinary share of brains) as to the propriety of Master Crustcrackit's shot, some alleging that he had played it off the cloth, others defending. The miller grew furiously warm.

'Ye wee, sneck-drawin' tailor-body, wad ye set up your bit feckless[1] face against a man o' place and siller?'

'Haud your tongue, miller,' cried one. 'Ye've nae cause to speak ill o' the way God made a man.'

Master Crustcrackit, however, needed no defender. He was ready in a second.

'And what dae ye ca' yoursel' but a great, God-forsaken dad o' a man, wi' a name like Braid Law and a mouth like the bottomless pit for yill[2] and beer and a manner o' carnal bakemeats. You to speak abune your breath to me,' and he hopped round his antagonist like an enraged fighting cock.

---

[1] lacking in energy          [2] ale

What the miller would have said no one may guess, had not a middle-aged man, who had been sitting on a settle placidly smoking a long white pipe, come up to see what was the dispute. He was dressed in a long black coat, with small-clothes of black, and broad silver-buckled shoon. The plain white cravat round his neck marked him for a minister.

'William Laverlaw and you, Peter Crustcrackit, as the minister of this parish, I command ye to be silent. I will have no disturbance on this public green. Nay, for I will adjudge your difference myself.'

All were silent in a second, and a hush of interest fell on the place.

'But that canna be,' grumbled the miller, 'for ye're nae great hand at the bowls.'

The minister stared sternly at the speaker, who sank at once into an aggrieved quiet. 'As God has appointed me the spiritual guide of this unworthy town, so also has He made me your master in secular affairs. I will settle your disputes and none other. And, sir, if you or any other dare gainsay me, then I shall feel justified in leaving argument for force, and the man who offends I shall fling into the Cuddie's Pool for the clearing of his brain and the benefit of his soul.' He spoke in a slow, methodical tone, rolling the words over his tongue. Then I remembered the many stories I had heard of this man's autocratic rule over the folk of the good town of Peebles; how he, alien alike to Whig and prelatist, went on his steadfast path caring for no man and snapping his fingers at the mandates of authority. And indeed in the quiet fierce face and weighty jaws there was something which debarred men from meddling with their owner.

Such was his influence on the people that none dared oppose him, and he gave his decision, which seemed to me to be a just and fair one. After this they fell to their play once more.

Meantime I had been looking on at the sport from the vantage ground of the low wall which looked down on the river. I had debated a question of farriery with the surgeon, who was also something of a horse doctor; and called out greetings to the different players, according as I favoured their colours. Then when the game no longer amused me, I had fallen to looking over the country down to the edge of the water where the small thatched cottages were yellow in the heat, and away up the broad empty channel to the Tweed. The cauld, where salmon leap in the spring and autumn and which is the greatest cauld on the river unless it be the one at Melrose, might have been crossed dryshod. I began to hate the weariful, everlasting glare and sigh for the clouds once more, and the soft turf and the hazy sky-line. Now it was so heavily oppressive that a man could scarcely draw a free breath. The players dripped with sweat and looked nigh exhausted, and for myself the sulphurous air weighed on me like a mount of lead and confused such wits as I had.

Even as I looked I saw a strange thing on the river bank which chained my languid curiosity. For down the haugh, swinging along at a great pace, came a man, the like of whom I had seldom seen. He ran at a steady trot more like a horse than a human creature, with his arms set close by his sides and without bonnet or shoes. His head swung from side to side with excessive weariness, and even at that distance I could see how he panted. In a trice he was over Peebles Water and had ascended the bank to the bowling green, cleared the low dyke, and stood gaping before us. Now I saw him plainer, and I have rarely seen a stranger sight. He seemed to have come a great distance, but no sweat stood on his brow, only a dun copper colour marking the effect of the hot sun. His breeches were utterly ragged and in places showed his long supple limbs. A shock of black hair covered his head and shaded his swarthy face. His eyes were wild and keen as a hawk's, and his tongue hung out of his mouth like a dog's in a chase. Every man stopped his play and looked at the queer newcomer. A whisper went round the place that it was that 'fule callant frae Brochtoun' but this brought no news to me.

The man stood still for maybe three minutes with his eyes fixed on the ground as if to recover breath. Then he looked up with dazed glances, like one wakening from sleep. He stared at me, then at the players, and burst into his tale, speaking in a high, excited voice.

'I hae run frae Drummeller to bring ye word. Quick, and get the folk out o' the waterside hooses or the feck[1] o' the toun'll be soomin'[2] to Berwick in an 'oor.'

No one spoke, but all stared as if they took him for a madman.

'There's been an awfu' storm up i' the muirs,' he went on, panting. 'And Tweed's comin' doon like a mill-race. The herd o' Powmood tellt me, and I got twae 'oors start o't and cam off here what I could rin. Get the folk out o' the water-side hooses when I bid ye, wi' a' their gear and plenishing, or there'll be no sae muckle as a groat's worth left by nicht. Up wi' ye and haste, for there's nae time to lose. I heard the roar o' the water miles off, louder than ony thunderstorm and mair terrible than an army wi' banners. Quick, ye doited bodies, if ye dinna want to hae mourning and lamentation i' the toun o' Peebles.'

At last, as you may believe, a great change passed over all. Some made no words about it, but rushed into the town to give the alarm; others stared stupidly as if waiting for more news; while some were disposed to treat the whole matter as a hoax. This enraged the newsbearer beyond telling. Springing up, he pointed to the western sky, and far off we saw a thick blackness creeping up the sky-line. 'If ye'll no believe me,' said he, 'will ye believe the finger o' God?' The word and the sight convinced the most distrusting.

Now Tweed, unlike all the other rivers of my knowledge, rises terribly at the first rain and travels slowly, so that Tweedsmuir may be under five feet of water and Peebles high and dry. This makes the whole valley a place of exceeding danger in sultry weather, for no man knows when a thunderstorm may break in

[1] most          [2] here, drifting

the hills and send the stream down a raging torrent. This, too, makes it possible to hear word of a flood before it comes, and by God's grace to provide against it.

The green was soon deserted. I rushed down to the waterside houses, which were in the nearest peril, and in shorter time than it takes to tell we had the people out and as much of their belongings as were worth saving; then we hastened to the low-lying cottages on Tweed Green and did likewise. Some of the folk seemed willing to resist, because, as they said, 'Whae kenned but that the body micht be a leear and they werena to hae a' this wark for naething?' For the great floods were but a tradition, and only the old men had seen the ruin which a spate could work. Nevertheless, even these were convinced by a threatening sky and a few words from the newsbearer's trenchant tongue. Soon the High Street and the Wynds were thick with household belongings, and the Castle Hill was crowded with folk to see the coming of the flood.

By this time the grim line of black had grown over half the sky, and down fell great drops of rain into the white, sun-baked channel. It was strange to watch these mighty splashes falling into the little stagnant pools and the runlets of flowing water. And still the close, thick heat hung over all, and men looked at the dawnings of the storm with sweat running over their brows. With the rain came a mist—a white ghastly haze which obliterated the hills and came down nigh to the stream. A sound, too, grew upon our ears, at first far away and dim, but increasing till it became a dull hollow thunder, varied with a strange, crackling, swishing noise which made a man eerie to listen to. Then all of a sudden the full blast of the thing came upon us. Men held their breaths as the wind and rain choked them and drove them back. It was scarce possible to see ahead, but the outlines of the gorge of Neidpath fleeted through the drift, whence the river issued. Every man turned his eyes thither and strained them to pierce the gloom.

Suddenly round the corner of the hill appeared a great yellow wave crested with white foam and filling the whole space. Down it came roaring and hissing, mowing the pines by the waterside as a reaper mows down hay with a scythe. Then with a mighty bound it broke from the hill barriers and spread over the haugh. Now the sound was like the bubbling of a pot ere it boils. We watched it in terror and admiration, as it swept on its awful course. In a trice it was at the cauld, and the cauld disappeared under a whirl of foam; now it was on the houses, and the walls went in like nutshells and the rubble was borne onward. A cry got up of, 'The bridge!' and all hung in wonder as it neared the old stonework, the first barrier to the torrent's course, the brave bridge of Peebles. It flung itself on with fiendish violence, but the stout mason-work stood firm, and the boiling tide went on through the narrow arches, leaving the bridge standing unshaken, as it had stood against many a flood. As we looked, we one and all broke into a cheer in honour of the old masons who had made so trusty a piece of stone.

I found myself in the crowd of spectators standing next to the man who had brought the tidings. He had recovered his breath and was watching the sight with a look half of interest and half of vexation. When all was past and only the turbid river remained, he shook himself like a dog and made to elbow his way out. 'I maun be awa',' he said, speaking to himself, 'and a sair job I'll hae gettin' ower Lyne Water.' When I heard him, I turned round and confronted him. There was something so pleasing about his face, his keen eyes, and alert head, that I could not forbear from offering him my hand, and telling him of my admiration for his deed. I was still but a boy and he was clearly some years my elder, so I made the advance, I doubt not, with a certain shyness and hesitancy. He looked at me sharply and smiled.

'Ye're the young laird o' Barns,' said he; 'I ken ye weel though ye maybe are no acquaint wi' me. I'm muckle honoured, sir, and gin ye'll come Brochtoun-ways sometime and speir for Nicol Plenderleith, he'll tak ye tae burns that were never fished afore and hills that never heard the sound o' a shot.'

I thanked him, and watched him slipping through the crowd till he was lost to view. This was my first meeting with Nicol Plenderleith, of whose ways and doings this tale will have much to say. The glamour of the strange fellow was still upon me as I set myself to make my road home. I am almost ashamed to tell of my misfortunes; for after crossing the bridge and riding to Manor Water, I found that this stream likewise had risen and had not left a bridge in its whole course. So I had to go up as far as St. Gordian's Cross before I could win over it, and did not reach Barns till after midnight, where I found my father half-crazy with concern and Tam Todd making ready to go and seek me.

*from* JOHN BURNET OF BARNS

# JOHN AND JEAN LANG

## DANDY JIM THE PACKMAN

· · ◦ · ·

It was the back end of the year. The crops were all in, but little was left of the harvest moon that had seen the Kirn safely won on the farms up 'Ousenam' Water. A disjaskit creature she looked as the wind drove a scud of dark cloud across her pale face, or when she peered over the black bank below her, only to be hidden once more by an angry drift of rain. It was no night for lonely wayfarers. Oxnam and Teviot were both in spate, and their moan could be heard when the wind rested for a little and allowed the fir trees to be still. Only for very short intervals, however, did the tireless wind cease, and always, after a short respite, the trees were attacked again, and made to beck and bow their dark heads like the nodding plumes of a hearse. The road from Crailing was in places dour with mud, heavy-rutted by harvest carts, with ever and anon a great puddle that stretched across from ditch to ditch. But dismal or not dismal, the night had apparently no evil effect on the spirits of the one man who was trudging his homeward way from Crailing to Eckford.

Dandy Jim, the packman, was a young fellow who wanted more than evil weather and a dreich, black night to depress him. A fine, upstanding lad he was, with a glib English tongue that readily sold his wares, and which, along with a handsome, merry face, helped him with ease into the good graces of those whom he familiarly knew as 'the lasses'. Dandy Jim had had many a flirtation, but now he felt that his roving days were nearly past. He was seriously thinking of matrimony.

'She's a bonny lass,' thought he contemplatively, dwelling on the charms of the young cook at the farmhouse he had left just past midnight, 'bonny and thrifty, and as fond o' a laugh as I am mysel. That bit shop as ye come out o' Hexham, with red roses growing up the front o't, and fine-scented laylock bushes at the back, that would do us fine. . . .'

And so, safely wrapped up in happy plans and in thoughts of his apple-cheeked lady-love, Jim manfully splashed through puddles and tramped through mud, conscience free, and fearful of nothing in earth or out of it. The graveyard at Eckford possessed no horrors for him. 'Bogles,' quoth he, 'what's a bogle? I threw muckle Sandy, the wrestler, at Lammas Fair, an' pity the bogle that meddles wi' me.'

But nevertheless, Jim, glancing towards the old church with its surrounding tomb-stones as he went by, saw something he did not expect, and quickly checked the defiant whistle that is, somehow, an infallible aid to the courage of even the bravest. There was a light over there among the graves, a flickering light that the wind lightly tossed, and that, somehow, did not suggest likeable things, even to Dandy Jim. Stock-still he stood for a couple of minutes watching the yellow glimmer among the tomb-stones, and then, with grim suspicion in his mind, he walked up to the churchyard gate. Nowadays we have only an occasional 'watchtower' in an old kirkyard, or a rusted iron cage over a grass-grown grave to remind us of times when human hyaenas prowled abroad after nightfall, and carried off their white, cold prey to be chaffered for by surgeons for the dissecting-rooms. But Dandy Jim's day was the day of Burke and Hare, of Dr. Knox, and of many another murderous and scientific ghoul, and a lantern's gleam in a churchyard in the small hours usually meant but one thing. As he expected, a gig stood at the churchyard gate; a bony, strong-shouldered, chestnut mare tethered to the gate-post, munching, mouth in nose-bag. In the gig was a sack, standing upright—a remarkably tall sack, five foot ten high at least, stiffly balanced against the seat.

'Aye, aye,' said Jim to himself, 'it was a six-foot coffin when they planted Jock the day. Him an' me was much of an age and of a height, poor lad; and here he is now, off to Edinburgh to be made mincemeat of.'

But even as he thought, he acted. The mare threw up an inquiring head as she felt a light step in the gig, and a sudden lightening of her load. But the wind wailed round the church and the rain beat down, dimming the glass in the flickering lantern, and every now and then Jim could hear a pick striking against a stone or a heavy thud as of a spadeful of damp earth being beaten down. Out of the gig came the sack, and out of the sack speedily came the packman's erstwhile acquaintance, Jock. A gap in the hedge across the road conveniently accom-modated Jock's unresisting body, over he went into the next field, and once again the mare started as Dandy Jim sprang into the gig with one bound and quickly struggled into the empty sack. He was only just in time. A parting clatter of pick-axe and a thud of spade, a swing of the lantern, that sent a yellow light athwart some grey old headstones, rough voices and hasty steps, and two men appeared, pushed their implements into the back of the gig, released the mare from her nose-bag, clambered in, and drove off at a quick trot.

For some time they proceeded in silence.

'A good haul,' at last one man remarked; 'a young chap—in fine condition.'

'A heavy load for the little mare,' said he who held the reins; 'fifteen stone if he's a pound. Not an easy one to tackle afore he died for want o' breath.'

Packman Jim lurched against the speaker ere the words were well out of his mouth. With an oath the man shoved him back, and Jim stiffly leaned against the seat in as nearly the attitude of the corpse, to whom he was acting as understudy, as he was able to assume. They had got a little beyond Kalefoot, and the flooded river was sending its moaning voice above the sough of the wind and the drip of the rain when one of the men spoke again to his companion. His voice was husky, and he spoke in a low tone as though he feared some eavesdropper.

'Before God, man,' he said, 'I can feel the body moving.'

The other, in his voice all the horror of a dread he had been trying to hide, answered in a shrill scream, 'It's warm, I tell ye!—the corpse is warm!'

Then came Dandy Jim's opportunity. His face was white enough in the uncertain glimmer of the gig's lamps when he thrust his head out of the sack and looked first at one and then at another of his companions. In a deep and hollow voice he spoke:

'If you had been where I hae been, your body would burn too,' said he.

A screech and a roar were, according to Dandy Jim, the result of his remark, and on either side of the gig a man cast himself out into the darkness, the rain, and the mud, and ran—ran—in heedless terror for an unknown sanctuary. What happened to the pair no subsequent historian has recorded but when Dandy

Jim shortly afterwards wed an apple-cheeked cook and took up his abode in a rose-covered cottage near Hexham, he no longer trudged the Border roads with a pack on his back, but drove a useful gig, drawn by a very willing, strong-shouldered, chestnut mare.

*from* STORIES OF THE BORDER MARCHES

## A. J. CRONIN

### THE TAY BRIDGE DISASTER

· · ✳ · ·

A SIGH broke from him as, slowly, the train drew to a standstill at a wayside station. The train, which was not express, had already made several halts at intermediate stations without his having particularly observed them, but here, to his annoyance, the door of his compartment opened and an old countryman entered. He seated himself blandly in the opposite corner, steaming from the rain, whilst puddles of water ran off him on to the cushions and floor; emanating from him, and mingling with the steam, came the spirituous odour of a liquid more potent than rain-water. Denis stared at him, then remarked coldly: 'This is a first-class compartment.'

The old fellow took a large red and white spotted handkerchief from his pocket and blew his nose like a trumpet.

''Deed it is,' he said solemnly, affecting to look round the carriage. 'I'm glad you told me. It's a rale pleasure for me to travel in style; but the first-class that ye speak o' doesna make muckle difference to me, for I havena got a ticket at all;' and he laughed uproariously, in a tipsy fashion.

Denis was so far below his normal humour that he failed to

appreciate the situation. In the ordinary way he would have amused himself intensely with this unexpected travelling-companion, but now he could only gaze at him glumly.

'Are you going far?' he finally asked.

'To Dundee—bonnie Dundee. The town ye ken—not the man. Na! Na! I'm not thinking o' the bonnets o' bonnie Dundee—I mean the bonnie town o' Dundee,' the other replied, and having thus explained himself with a grave and scrupulous exactitude, he added, meaningly: 'I hadna time to get my ticket, though.'

Denis sat up. He would, he realized, have to endure this for the rest of the journey, and he resigned himself to it.

'What's the weather like now?' he asked. 'You look wet!'

'Wet! I'm wet outside and inside. But the one counteracts the other, ye ken, and to a hardy shepherd like me wet clothes just means lettin' them dry on ye. But mind ye, it is a most awful, soughin' night all the same. I'm glad I'm not out on the hills.'

He nodded his head several times, took a small, foul stump of clay pipe from his pocket, lit it, covered it with its metal cap, and, inverting it from the corner of his mouth, sucked noisily; when he had filled the carriage with smoke, he spat copiously upon the floor without removing the pipe from his mouth.

Denis looked at the other with compassionate disgust, and as he tried to picture this gross, bibulous old yokel as a young man, then wondered moodily if he himself might ever degenerate to such a crapulous old age, his melancholy grew more profound. Unconscious of the effect he had produced, the old shepherd continued: 'Ah! It's good-bye to the hills for me. That sounds kind o' well, think ye no'? Ay! Good-bye to the hills. Man!'—he laughed, slapping his thigh—'It's like the name o' a sang. Good-bye to the Hills. Weel, onyway, I'm going back to my native town, and you'll never guess what for.' He tittered vehemently, choking himself with smoke.

'You've come into some money, perhaps?' hazarded Denis.

''Deed, no! The bit of money I've got is what I've saved by

hard and honest work. Try again.' As Denis remained silent he went on, garrulously.

'Ay! you'd never think it, but the plain truth is that I'm going—' He paused to wink prodigiously, then blurted out, 'I'm goin' to Dundee to get married.' Observing with manifest enjoyment the effect he had produced, he meandered on—

'I'm a hardy blade, although I'm not so souple as I was, and there's a fine, sonsie woman waiting for me. She was a great friend of my first wife. Ay! I'm to wed early in the morn's mornin'. That's the way I'm takin' this train and breakin' the Sabbath. I maun be in time, ye ken.'

As the other wandered on, Denis gazed at him with a curious repulsion, due, in the main, to the strange coincidence of his own circumstances. Here, then, was another bridegroom, linked to him in this narrow compartment by a bond of corresponding position. Did this disreputable veteran mirror the image of his contumely, or reflect to him a dolorous premonition of his future?

In dismay Denis asked himself if he were not as contemptible in the eyes of his own kind as this grey-beard was in his. A tide of self-depreciation and condemnation rushed over him as he began to review the manner of his life. An unusual humility startled him by the rapidity and force of its onset, and in this despair he remained, subdued and silent, until the train clattered into the station of St. Fort. Here his companion rose and got out of the compartment, remarking, as he did so: 'We've a good way to go yet. I'll just get out and see if I canna get haud o' something to keep out the cauld. Just a wee dram to warm the inside o' the stammack.' In a moment, however, he came back, to say reassuringly: 'I'll be back! I'm not away, mind ye. I wouldna leave ye like that. I'll be back to keep ye company till we get to Dundee.' Then he tramped off.

Denis looked at his watch and saw that it was five minutes past seven. The train was up to time, yet, as he put his head out of the window, he found that the strength of the wind had increased beyond endurance. Passengers getting out of the open doors were bowled along the platform, and the heavy train, as it stood stationary, seemed to rock upon its wheels. Surrounding McBeath he saw a wind-beaten group clamouring: 'Is it safe for us to gang on, guard?'

'What a wind it is! Will the train stand it?'

'Will it keep on the line?'

'Lord, save us, what a night it is! What about the bridge? Oh! I wish we were a' hame!'

He thought his friend the guard looked perturbed and irritable but although McBeath did indeed feel anxious, with the charge of a hundred people upon his mind, he maintained in his replies the even and imperturbable calm of officialdom.

'Safe as the Bank of Scotland, ma'am.'

'Wind forsooth! Tuts, it's only a bit breezie, man. Think shame o' yourself.'

'Ay, it'll haud the line and ye'll be hame wi' your lassock in an hour, ma fine wumman!' Denis heard him repeat placidly, composedly, impenetrably. His calmness seemed to reassure them completely, and at his comforting words the people broke up and entered their compartments.

At length the all clear was given and the train again began to move. As it did so Denis observed the figure of his travelling companion staggering against the wind in an effort to attain the rearmost carriage, but in his anxiety and haste, the old shepherd slipped and fell prostrate upon the platform. The train drew away from him, he was irrevocably left behind, and, as they moved out of the station, Denis caught a last glimpse, under the flicker of the station lamp, of the perplexed, discomfited face, filled with almost ludicrous desolation. As he sat in his corner, while the train approached the southern edge of the Tay Bridge, Denis reflected with a sombre humour that the other would assuredly be late for his nuptials in the morning. Perhaps it was a lesson meant for him. Yes, he must profit by this strange, unpleasant coincidence. He would not fail Mary on Tuesday!

The train moved on and, at thirteen minutes past seven, it reached the beginning of the bridge. At this point, before entering upon the single line of rails over the bridge, it slowed down opposite the signal cabin, to allow the baton to be passed. Without this exchange it was not permitted to proceed, and, still filled by a sense of misgiving, Denis again lowered his window and looked out, to observe that everything was correct. The force of the gale almost decapitated him but, in the red glare cast by the engine, he discerned, stretching dimly into the distance, the massive girders of the bridge, like the colossal skeleton of an enormous reptile, but of steel, strong and adamantine. Then, all at once, he saw the signalman descend the steps from his box with consummate care, clutching the rail tightly with one hand. He surrendered the baton to the stoker, and, when he had accomplished this, he climbed back into his cabin with the utmost difficulty, fighting the wind and being assisted up the last few steps by the hand of a friend held out to him from within.

And now the train moved off again, and entered the bridge. Denis raised his window and sank back in his seat composedly, but, as he was carried past the signal-box, he received the fleeting impression of two pale, terrified faces looking at him out of it, like ghostly countenances brushing past him in the blackness.

The violence of the gale was now unbounded. The wind hurled the rain against the sides of the train with the noise of a thousand anvils, and the wet snow again came slobbering upon the window panes, blotting out all vision. The train rocked upon the rails with a drunken, swaying oscillation, and although it proceeded slowly, cautiously, it seemed, from the fury and rush of the storm, to dash headlong upon its course. Thus, as it advanced, with the blackness, the noise of the wheels, the tearing rush of the wind, and the crashing of the waves upon the pier of the bridge below, there was developed the sensation of reckless, headlong acceleration.

As Denis sat alone, in the silent, cabined space of his compartment, tossed this way and that by the jactation, he felt suddenly that the grinding wheels of the train spoke to him. As they raced upon the line he heard them rasp out, with a heavy, despairing refrain: 'God help us! God help us! God help us!'

Amidst the blare of the storm this slow, melancholy dirge beat itself into Denis's brain. The certain sense of some terrible disaster began to oppress him. Strangely, he feared not for himself, but for Mary. Frightful visions flashed through the dark field of his imagination. He saw her, in a white shroud, with sad, imploring eyes, with dank, streaming hair, with bleeding feet and hands. Fantastic shapes oppressed her which made her shrink into the obliterating darkness. Again he saw her grimacing, simpering palely like a sorry statue of the Madonna and holding by the hand the weazened figure of a child. He shouted in horror. In a panic of distress he jumped to his feet. He desired to get to her. He wanted to open the door, to jump out of this confining box which enclosed him like a sepulchre. He would have given, instantly, everything he possessed to get out of the train. But he could not.

He was imprisoned in the train, which advanced inexorably, winding in its own glare like a dark, red serpent twisting sinuously forward. It had traversed one mile of the bridge and had now reached the middle span, where a mesh of steel girders formed a hollow tube through which it must pass. The train entered this tunnel. It entered slowly, fearfully, reluctantly, juddering in every bolt and rivet of its frame as the hurricane assaulted, and sought to destroy, the greater resistance now offered to it. The wheels clanked with the ceaseless insistence of the tolling of a passing-bell, still protesting, endlessly: 'God help us! God help us! God help us!'

Then, abruptly, when the whole train lay enwrapped within

the iron lamellae of the middle link of the bridge, the wind elevated itself with a culminating, exultant roar to the orgasm of its power and passion.

The bridge broke. Steel girders snapped like twigs, cement crumbled like sand, iron pillars bent like willow wands. The middle span melted like wax. Its wreckage clung around the tortured train, which gyrated madly for an instant in space. Immediately, a shattering rush of broken glass and wood descended upon Denis, cutting and bruising him with mangling violence. He felt the wrenching torsion of metal, and the grating of falling masonry. The inexpressible desolation of a hundred human voices, united in a sudden, short, anguished cry of mingled agony and terror, fell upon his ears hideously, with the deathly fatality of a coronach. The walls of his compartment whirled about him and upon him, like a winding-sheet, the floor rushed over his head. As he spun round, with a loud cry he, too, shouted: 'God help us!' then, faintly, the name: 'Mary!'

Then the train with incredible speed, curving like a rocket, arched the darkness in a glittering parabola of light, and plunged soundlessly into the black hell of water below, where, like a rocket, it was instantly extinguished—for ever obliterated! For the infinity of a second, as he hurtled through the air, Denis knew what had happened. He knew everything, then instantly he ceased to know. At the same instant as the first, faint cry of his child ascended feebly in the byre at Levenford, his mutilated body hit the dark, raging water and lay dead, deep down upon the bed of the firth.

*from* HATTER'S CASTLE

# GEORGE BLAKE

## THE FIRST TRAIN IN GARVEL

. . * . .

A LINE of red-coated militiamen held the mob away from the lowest step of the fine broad flight which led up to the new railway station. The officer in charge, the heavy scabbard of his curved sword clattering on the granite, came along the row to look at a white card waved in the outstretched hand of a tall young gentleman with a lady on his arm. As he reached out for the oblong of the cardboard, his hand and forearm heavily gauntleted in white leather, the dark eyes of the officer took in the facts that the young man in fawn trousers and dark blue cutaway coat was indubitably a person of social standing, and that the young lady he escorted was well-favoured beyond the ordinary. Canvassing her charms in the masculine intimacy of the ante-room, the gallant subaltern would assuredly have described them in ebullient terms.

Now, on parade, he returned the card to its bearer with a bow and permitted himself just the ghost of a hopeful smile towards the lady. (He was always conscious, that young man, of his own dark, romantic eyes under dark, rich eyebrows.) He clicked his heels, bowed again, and saluted. The lady bowed in return, the young gentleman raised his tall hat, and, amid the sardonic cheers of the common folk still held outside the barrier, Dr. Walter Oliphant of Goldenhaddock and Miss Phoebe Craufurd of Kilblain proceeded, not unlike figures in a stage scene, up the flight of steps and so out of sight of the mob through the gates of the new railway's western terminus.

After the noisy huddle of the public approach to it, the station seemed to be part of quite another sort of world. The designers of the place had contrived to give it that troglodyte atmosphere which hangs about every railway enterprise to this day. The line of rails had the air of resting in an excavation. A canopy over the platform, its eaves fringed with decorative ironwork, conspired with the blank wall of a shed beyond the rails to make of the station a sort of hall of echoes. It was a day of late March, inordinately mild in the season of growth, but even the sunlight of early afternoon fell in shafts between canopy and shed as if through the windows of a prison.

Like a child at an exhibition Miss Craufurd exclaimed at everything, pointing out this and that novelty to her escort with eager motions of the parasol she dared to carry in this early week of the Scottish year.

'And aren't we the lucky ones, Walter?' she cried. 'But, look! Most of our friends are here already.'

They were among the lucky ones, indeed, but not quite the luckiest of all. It was a very select company that had been cheered out of Garvel an hour before noon that day—to martial music and a booming of cannon in the first train of twelve carriages, drawn by two engines, to depart for the city, twenty-odd miles away, along the wonderful new track laid down at vast expense and in daring defiance of natural and legal obstacles innumerable. The parents of Miss Craufurd and the parents of Dr. Walter Oliphant were of that highly privileged party which had been whisked away on the glittering wings of invention, and those of the younger generation and of the slightly lower orders who now awaited their return were in a second order of precedence, although vastly exalted above the eager, sardonic mob of the common folk that milled companionably in the station approaches.

Miss Craufurd and Dr. Oliphant were not, however, in the least affected by any awareness of subtle degradation. Their quite natural feeling, even in that age of mercantile expansion, was stoutly feudal. Their parents, representing their established families, had departed into space on a bold and possibly dangerous excursion in the van of progress. They were well content as young folk to be privileged to assemble for the high purpose of greeting the returning voyagers, pioneers triumphant. The military band was there at the eastern end of the platform, ready to strike up *See the Conquering Hero* at a moment's warning. The guns of a regiment of artillery were primed to fire a salute.

With a little bow of formality, Dr. Oliphant offered to his fair charge the oblong of cardboard which had gained them admission to this enclosure.

'You might care to have this card as a souvenir, Phoebe,' he suggested.

'But how charming, Walter!' cried the young lady, who had been finished at a convent in Brussels. 'Look! It has your uncle's own signature! "Mark Oliphant, Director." Oh, I shall keep this among my dearest possessions!'

Railway or no railway, Walter would have found the company of Miss Craufurd enough for any hour. They were but a month betrothed, and this girl of nineteen, the youngest of a famously handsome family, glowed like a flower in the sun of love and triumph. Her morning dress, with its domed skirt, was of peacock green shot with purple; over her shoulders with the tight bodice was draped a long Paisley shawl, white with an edging to match the dress. A purple bonnet in the candid fashion of the period exquisitely framed two ringlets of her hair, and within that second dark frame the girl's lovely oval face, flawless in cream and blush, had the beauty of all the dawns and springtides of the world.

This handsome couple, for tall young Dr. Oliphant fairly matched the lady in his own masculine and faintly severe manner of looks, was warmly greeted by those already on the station platform. There were many of their own generation to salute them as having so elegantly, nay so perfectly, reached the decision proper to their age and eligibility. There were still more in the inferior grades of society—the comfortable, sentimental wives of the more substantial shopkeepers, for instance, and their uneasily envious daughters—to overwhelm them with effusiveness. As they came up with the main party, the band of music at the end of the platform chose, with a nice, accidental touch of theatricality, to fill in the waiting time with a selection and burst valiantly into one of the new and nearly licentious Viennese waltzes.

So, amid a continuous chatter of female greetings and exclamations, with dark undertones of grave male prognostications as to the effect of the new railway communication on the trade of the town, the time of waiting passed quickly. A detached listener from another age might have picked up as significant such words and phrases as: coal, redingote, prosperity, pelerine, figured, grenadine, screw, water, mantlet, iron, tides, three-fold linen buttons, villas, assembly, steam-boat, and again coal; but those who uttered them had no such sense of significance, even if the men among them were cast in the grave mould of those who consciously see destiny in the shaping. They were just men and women of 1841, waiting for the first train to return to Garvel and to applaud an agreeable phenomenon.

Its approach was intimated by the murmur of distant cheering up the line, echoed from the Hillend slopes. The more observant and sharp-eyed watchers noted the gyrations of boys on trees, walls, and roof-tops along the curving track to the eastward. The military band was seen to pick up and assume in readiness its formidable instruments. The company on the platform, like a company of infantry at drill, turned half-left. There the brave wreaths of smoke and steam were seen rising in puffs behind the cottages at Anglestone; and in that single space of interminable time, no more than fifteen seconds altogether, the cheers of greeting started to rise from between thousands of lips, the battery of guns began to boom, and Mr. Handel's neat march saluted still another event more fantastic than the composer ever dreamed of.

On the people waiting at the terminus the near approach of the train created a profound impression of might. The gleaming brass of the two locomotives, the hiss and pulse of compressed steam, the gigantic hoops of the driving wheels, the scream of brakes and the jolting of carriages—all these sights and sounds conveyed an exciting impression of enormous power successfully controlled by gifted members of the remarkable species to which they themselves belonged. The forward surge to greet the historic survivors of the experiment was a miracle of happy unanimity.

To the clinically observant eye of Dr. Walter Oliphant, at least, it did not appear that the travellers had made the journey without discomfort. The faces of the men among them were begrimed to a greater or less extent, their eyelids inflamed. It was to be noted that most of the ladies descending from the train shook their mantles or shawls with irritable little gestures or impatiently flicked fragments of cinder from their sleeves and gloves. Those who had guarded themselves with parasols twirled them like tops on the platform.

Such small gestures, however, were largely unconscious and passed nearly unnoticed in the excitement of the monstrous event. The air was loud, even above the hiss of steam, with cries and greetings and congratulations and prophecies.

'Prodigious! Only 65 minutes from the city—24 miles! We shall be flying next! I declare I had to hold my bonnet on all the time! The trees seemed to fly past! It seems like a year since we left Garvel this morning. I declare I'll waken up and find it is all a dream! Now we can count on unlimited supplies of coal at a really reasonable rate! This, sir, spells the end of riverborne traffic!'

*from* THE CONSTANT STAR

# CONTEMPORARY PANORAMA

## FACT

# WILLIAM POWER

## STORM, SUN, AND SHOWER

. . * . .

THE starry heavens, and the moral law in the heart of man, seemed to Kant the most impressive things in the universe. The sky on a clear moonless night in early winter is the very thing in nature that strikes a city-bred man who has gone to live in the open uplands.

The majestic spread of the Plough, the gem-like brilliance of Orion, the glittering swarm of the Pleiades, move him to admiration. He has only read of the Milky Way: now he beholds it, a mighty fountain-arch of luminous dust, stretching overhead across the sky, breaking into two streams as it falls. He is puzzled by bright lights close down to the very horizon, where in the city there is only a sulphurous dimness. They are stars!

In time he notices the difference between the hard sparkle of the stars on a still, frosty night, their blown and washed appearance in a north-west gale, and their liquid softness in clear, moist spells, 'when stars are weeping'. And he recalls Rousseau's inspired word for the secular stellar movement—'deploying'— and, in a kind of awed despair, murmurs, 'The heavens declare the glory of God; and the firmament sheweth His handywork.'

Sunset is an expansion of wonder already glimpsed, but a vast, blood-red dawn over slopes of snow, cold purple, with rose sparkles, is a revelation.

On a bright mild morning in April, after a week of tepid smirr succeeding frost, he looks out over the valley to the huge stretch of meadow and moorland that for months has been tawny and dull. This morning it is like the plains and hills of heaven, a shimmering expanse of light green and silver, miles on miles, with beacons of shining gold.

A constant wonder is the winter wind. In the city it merely whistles, shrieks, and bellows. Out on the forest ridge between valley and upland, its note is infinitely varied.

Last night the fading moon was greasy. Today, despite the clear air, the light almost failed, so thick was the blanket of drizzling cloud. The rooks have flown over early to their winter dormitory in the valley. The weather-wise remark that they are glad they have not to cross the Irish Sea tonight.

The evening darkness is thick and almost hot. Through its clammy folds comes a faint breathing, then a whistling and moaning, then a booming. Doors and window-frames creak. There is a pause of indecisive sighings and strainings. Then a moment of complete calm. The advance-guard has completed its reconnaissance, and fallen back on the main army.

Straining ears through the blackness, one hears, far down in the south-west valley, a sound like muffled thunder, or great distant waters fighting their way through choked canyons. The sound changes to a noise like Attila's cavalry debouching on the plain of Chalons. The viewless horsemen of the blast have broken cover, on a front of a hundred miles. They are thundering and bellowing up the slope. With a shriek and a yell they strike the house. The battle is let loose.

Nature cowers and quivers. The birds cling faster to the branches, and push their heads farther under their wings. The night-birds are silent. Bunnies dig deeper into their burrows. Tonight the weasels fast. The kennel-dog jumps out, gives a frightened bark and howl, and, with tail down, rushes back into his lodging and buries himself in the straw.

The gale rises and rises. The world lies prostrate. The whistling is constant and despairing. Fastenings of all kinds rattle. The surroundings of the house are disquietingly vocal. The chimneys boom. At the climaxes of the gale, other sounds are drowned by a thunderous drumming and roaring. The big guns are in action. One feels the slates lift, all at once. The south-wester has his fangs in us. He is shaking us as a dog shakes a rat. The general sensation is as if the house were suspended in the midst of the main fall of Niagara. Is the whole house really lifting? It can hardly resist that terrific aerial pressure.

Listening again, one can hear the successive cohorts of the storm galloping up the charge. When they have passed, one can hear them thundering away up into the north-east. Distant crashes and bangings bespeak the work of the hooves. The noise of heavy trains, throbbing up the incline or rattling down, is only intermittently audible; their whistlings are twisted and spun away.

The air, because of the sub-tropical latitudes from which the gale blows, and the rapid movement of the particles, is curiously warm. Thunder-and-lightning is very rare with a south-west gale; but millions of electrical discharges—invisible lightnings— create an absorbed luminosity, making darkness visible, and suffusing the eyes with a woolly mist. On such a night a wanderer in broken country would be stunned and overwhelmed, and would be in danger of coming to grief in an old quarry or a swollen stream.

Through all this tumultuous orchestration there runs a rich solemn music. Whenever the drums and tubas ease off, one hears the voluminous but muted theme given out by the strings and wood-winds of the forest. It is a beautiful rushing sound, like a multitude of rushing streams washing along in beds of varying composition and declivity. In the heart of pine-woods scarcely a draught is felt, and the rushing and whishing and tossing and surging overhead are like the noise of a great impetuous river, flowing over an enchanted cave. One thinks of Rheingold—and of the nursery rhymes of infancy—'Hush-a-bye, baby, on the tree-top'.

The noise and electric tension make sleep impossible. One's

thoughts follow the gale, across moorland and farmland, and the streaming and empty streets of the towns, where the lights flicker and glisten and the chimney-cowls whirl and scream; and over the hills and far away, down white-whipped estuaries to the boiling cauldron of the open sea, where steamers with sparks flying from their funnels plunge and smother in acres of ghostly foam, mingling with the breaking crests of the inexorable combers that tear it up as the horns of a mad bull might tear a web of lawn.

It is there on a night like this, that the high hearts of our race are steeled and tested. On those obstinately wallowing boxes of metal are the flower of mankind. They do not undervalue their adversary. Have you noticed the quiet contempt with which a sailor regards a landlubber who sighs for a snoring breeze, and the white waves heaving high? I shouldn't be ashamed to confess to an old salt that I was 'thankful to be at home on a night like this'.

*from* MY SCOTLAND

## MORAY McLAREN

### LOST IN THE HILLS

· · * · ·

THE night now began to fall in dead earnest, the wind increased, and, to my extreme discomfort, I noticed that the rain contained flakes of that uncomfortable mixture of snow and water. Even in summer on those heights in Ross-shire one is never quite free from the chance of a fall of snow. We stumbled on together, occasionally shouting and talking to keep our spirits up, and in an hour's time we reached the main stream of the valley. To our delight it proved easily fordable—we were far too wet and cold already to mind the wading—and, instead of continuing eastwards to where we knew the road curled round and over the bridge, we decided to make a short cut, and carry on north to meet it a little farther up. This turned out to be a most disheartening adventure. The mist and darkness were already far too thick around us or we would not have attempted it, for we would have seen what lay before us.

After crossing the stream we at once began to ascend; at no time could we see more than a hundred yards ahead of us; and so we had gone on for some considerable time before we understood that, far from crossing a simple bit of moorland lying between us and the road, we were scaling the side of a mountain. Neither of us dared to admit that we were beaten. We toiled on and on and up until, as the wisp of mist for one solitary moment separated itself from the main bulk of cloud, the last gleam of an ashen-grey twilight showed us to be standing under the lee of an immense crag, quite unscalable. Had I been alone, I would have burst into tears with the disappointment; as it was, we both turned and without any words to each other began the disgusting labour of retracing the course which we had taken in such hope. Down we went, careless now of twisting ankles and bruised elbows; all we wanted to do was to gain the valley again and continue our course to the east, where we knew the road lay. 'Fools, fools!' I kept murmuring to myself like some refrain, a habit of mine when I am tired and angry. 'Why did we trust that short cut?'

The descent took much less time than any other piece of walking we had done that day—we were getting anxious. When one is in a frightened hurry, one becomes surprisingly agile and goat-like on one's feet. I had been tired before, but now I began to get something of the second wind of my energy back again, and a strange lightness seemed to carry me easily forward over the most difficult boulders and gullies.

At last we reached the stream again, and, this time on its northern side, began to make our painful way up the glen. This was an extraordinarily foolish mistake for two Scotsmen to make. Any fool could have told us to keep to the high land, for the hills were full of the mournful roar of swollen streams. Every trickle was now, after five hours' drenching rain, a tempestuous cascade, and ordinary streams were, in this easily excitable country, great sluices of yellow foaming spate. All had as their end, all were tributary to, the main stream of the valley. And so, as any fool could have told us, we had to cross every stream that came from the northern side, at its widest and deepest point, that is, just before it joined the central stream.

I now began to wonder whether I should have the strength to reach the road; my second wind of energy proved to be a very transitory and weak thing. It had soon ebbed out of my stumbling, gasping body, and left me a prey to the shrieking winds and the coldest cold that I have ever endured. It was quite different from all other feelings of cold that I have felt. Others were superficial; this had quite literally seized me by the heart, and I could feel my blood had not the vigour to combat it. My bones were like sticks of ice and my bowels had no more warmth in them than had my skin.

Every few hundred feet we had to cross a torrent that was on its way to join the main stream beside which we were walking. We knew our mistake now, but had not the heart to set it right by climbing to the flank of that abominable hill again. All that we could do was to keep going on and on in one direction. We were quite careless of the way we crossed these streams, for every stitch of clothing we had on us was dripping (and you must remember that all I had was a shirt, a pair of flannel trousers, and my boots and socks), and we would, without any thought, walk straight into them, sometimes falling flat down in the water, sometimes stepping into holes that almost submerged us. All that we had the energy to do was to go on and on. The ground in between the streams was almost as bad. Thinking on it afterwards, I was glad that it was soft, for I am sure that we would have sprained our ankles or broken our legs had it been stony, but at the time this softness was maddening.

Now swampy, now covered with masses of heather, it was perpetually rising and falling; and could anyone have seen us, I think we would have made at the same time one of the most pitiful and most comical sights imaginable. We had long ceased to cry out or make any sign when we fell; we just scrambled on to our feet and dragged ourselves on. As we fell, we fell completely, quite flat down on our faces in the soft swamp or vegetation; and this happened on an average once every fifty yards. We moved like drunken men, or like children learning to walk on the counterpane of an immense bed. Sometimes one of us would be down three times in twenty yards; sometimes we would manage three hundred yards without a fall; but it was chance, not our circumspection, that would allow this. We were now quite careless of how we walked; all that we contrived to do was to keep moving on by the side of the now deepening and curving stream, splashing, falling, crawling rather than wading through its innumerable tributaries.

All this time I kept on trying to force my numbed brain to remember exactly the appearance of the map. I could see the shape of the valley as the map had drawn it, and I remembered that the stream was shown as winding in it just before it got to the bridge where the road ran over it. I could not, however, just remember the scale, or how long the valley was. I felt rather than knew that we must be near the road; we had clearly covered some miles of the valley and had been on the move for hours. The road simply could not be more than half a mile ahead of us now. The road began to assume in my mind a greater importance than that of the inn, the shelter, the food and wine. Those were too distant: they were unimaginable. The thing that we must reach, must see and feel before us was that road. The road would not be any more kind to us than this swamp. It would, indeed, be more uncomfortable to fall on the road than here; and the wind and rain would be just as cold there. It was just that the road was our immediate objective; it was the thing on which we had pinned our hopes; to reach it would be to have achieved something; it would be a proof that we were not just walking in a delirium. I didn't want to do anything with the road. I didn't know whether I could walk to Cluanie on the road, but somehow I felt that I could be content with the road. I could lie down and sleep on it, happy in the knowledge that I had got to it.

Then I began to notice a thing which I at first could not or would not believe, but which eventually became so obvious that hope died within me, and all my mind and body went alive again with fear. The stream on our right had for some time ceased to make any running sound, it had grown deep and slow, like an English river, and looked most unnatural in these moorland surroundings. I at last saw that not only had it ceased to make a noise, but it had stopped flowing altogether. We were no longer walking beside a stream, but upon the shores of a loch. We stopped and strained to look through the rain and darkness across the water. We could see no other side, and yet we could see far enough to understand that this was no stream or river. It was a great broad lake or long tarn lying stretched out upon what we now began to perceive was no valley but a great moorland desert all around. For shelter of the hills was withdrawn from us, the wind, the streaming clouds, the rain beat upon us now with nothing to protect us. And when the clouds in their hurry occasionally separated above our heads and let through enough weak light from the moon to show us our surroundings, all we could see was a waste of water on one side and of moor on the other. There had been no loch marked on the map, in the place where I had supposed we were, and there had been mountains on the other side. We were lost. The road was now for ever denied us.

It was now obvious to me that I should probably die before I could drag myself to any shelter. For the last hour or so, my mind had ever so distantly toyed with the idea that the exposure might be too much for me before Cluanie; but the road had become such an obsession, it was so immediately desirable, that the wish for it had pushed fear out of my mind. Now, when in a few seconds the hope of gaining the road was withdrawn from me, the realization of Death, accompanied by my extravagant fear of it, rushed in and occupied every nook and cranny of my mind. Through the confusion of the noise in my ear and the deadness of my numbed body and brain, there shot like an electric current the terror of annihilation. I was in an instant revivified, not into action, but into sensation. There was nothing to do save to walk on, and that seemed hopeless; the chances were hundreds to one that we would not come to any shelter before we collapsed.

Once off the road in this most desolate part of Scotland, I knew that one might walk for forty miles through valleys and over swamps, passing between small houses and villages a few miles on either side, but never seeing them. A moment before exhaustion and cold seemed to have robbed me of all power of consecutive thought. A vague sleepiness had obscured the process of my mind. Now, in a lightning flash of fear, I knew and clearly understood everything.

It would be tedious to go on describing the pain and fear of the next two hours. I had often before had to face for about five seconds the possibility of Death, as, for instance, when a motor accident seemed inevitable; but never before, and never again, I hope, shall I have to endure the close prospect of that abominable fact for two hours on end. I had been in the habit of trying to comfort myself when I had been more than usually worried by Death, by telling myself that when it came actually to dying, when one was really up against it, one would be given hope or faith or some triumphant emotion which would conquer terror. Whether this is not true, or whether hope was withheld from me because I was destined not to die on this occasion, I do not know; but certainly never in my life has my foolish terror more violently seized and tormented me than during these two hours.

We kept straight on in the direction we had been taking, and as the shore of the loch seemed quite straight we kept it on our right the whole time. We walked now, not so much with the hope of getting anywhere, but merely because we knew that if we didn't move we should fall asleep and die of cold and exposure. Sometimes we came to large boulders or a dip in the heather which gave a meagre little shelter and for about a hundred seconds my companion (who was the more vigorous and masterful of us) would allow me to stop. We would draw close during these pauses and put our arms round each other, so that we got an illusion of warmth from each other's bodies. Always a great longing for sleep came over me when we stopped like this, a longing which in no way took away from fear, but merely seemed to make it more uneasy and unconquerable, as in a nightmare. And when the strength and determination of my companion jerked me out of these half-slumbers, I would awake only to an equally uneasy realization of fact.

There is very little more of our walk that I can remember. Once I thought that we had stumbled upon the devil, for right before there rose a great figure not ten yards away. It plunged into the loch with an appalling splash and started to swim to the other side with its horns proudly raised above the water— we had disturbed a great red stag by the water side. Once I pretended to sprain my ankle so that I might force my companion to rest a little. He saw through my lie and shook me so hard that I was crying before he would stop and was convinced that I was awake enough to go on. These two incidents, and the first sight of a dreary grey dawn beginning ever so faintly to influence the weeping night, are the only things I can remember until my companion suddenly broke into what seemed to me a despairing maniacal run, leaving me to sink back into a dip in the heather where I stretched out, longing for nothing save sleep which I lyingly told myself would bring me strength.

I was being shaken again. Two people were pulling me to my feet. They were making me walk, at least, I suppose I was walking. It seemed to me that I just skimmed, like a mote of dust, over the surface of the ground. We were going through a door, and there were red lights about, and a woman's face was so close to me that I thought it was going to sink right into my brain, so I put out my hand to push it away, but it was already yards away from me. And then slowly (though with another part of my mind, I knew it only took about ten seconds) things swam back into focus. I was standing in a room. The main room of a croft. The lamps were lit. An old shepherd was holding my arm and half-tearing, half-peeling my clothes off me, while a woman was bending over the fireplace turning back the smouldering peat hags, so that the glowing sides were turned out to face the room. I tried to move towards the fire and when the shepherd held me back I remember that I began to speak in a stupid, loose, unintelligible kind of way, keeping on struggling to get nearer the fire.

The woman came up to me, and with the sighing, infinitely comfortable voice of the North, told me that I must not get near the fire.

'You are too colt. You may not come to the fire for a wee pit. You will be purnt. Na, na, you must be slow; it is not goot for you; it is not goot for you.'

She kept on saying these last words over and over again, less for their meaning than for their soothing repetition, while she helped her husband to take off my clothes. When I was stripped she dried me with a rough piece of cloth, and then very slowly allowed me to come nearer to the glow.

The pain of being warmed, ever so gently as these wise people would allow me, then gripped me, and I felt that slow relaxation of the muscles, half-frozen, numbed with exhaustion, which they had feared to let me endure too strongly at first. The woman then began to rub my limbs, to massage me with a mixture of warm water and whisky. Standing before her, naked as a child, with her rough hands all over me, with the pain of the influencing heat and the smell of the spirit in my brain, I could not help thinking of the absurd story of the refined English traveller who, having sprained his ankle on the moors, was having his foot and ankle washed in whisky by the proprietor of his hotel. He commented on the lavish way the whisky was being used and begged the proprietor not to waste it. 'Inteed, inteed, it is no waste whateffer,' replied the Highlandman, 'the shentlemen do often hurt their feet and it gives a beautiful flavour to the whisky.' I wondered whether my body would give a beautiful flavour to this whisky, and I started laughing in a silly kind of way.

They put me to bed somewhere in the croft. It was comfortable, but I was too tired to sleep easily, and until five o'clock in the afternoon I lay on the border line of a feverish slumber. At five she made me sit up and drink a great tumbler of hot milk, whereon I sweated in streams and then fell peacefully into a deep sleep until the next morning.

My friend who had much more strength than I had left the croft on the afternoon of the day we reached it and was shown the way back to Cluanie. So, as soon as I was ready to go back, the MacDonalds very kindly sent a car down to the point on the road nearest to the croft. I rode over on a pony with my host to meet it and could have cried with joy when I saw MacDonald's cheerful face again at the wheel. Instead, I told over and over again the story of our adventures and then told them once more to Mrs. MacDonald when I got back to Cluanie. . . . I had a magnificent dinner that night.

*from* RETURN TO SCOTLAND

# ALASTAIR M. DUNNETT

## THE DORUS MOR

. . * . .

*This was our time that we took—*
*We, on that day, and no others;*
*The wind was a friend for the look*
*He laid on the sail as it shook,*
*And the sea said—'Come then, brothers!'*

THE Dorus Mor (the Great Door) was likely to be our biggest
immediate difficulty. We knew of it already. Campbell the
Pilot had told us to pass it at slack water, but some local guidance
seemed desirable. It is a half-mile gap of water between the
mainland Point of Craignish and the island of Garbh Reisa. Here
the tide, running irregularly round the island and meeting in the
gap on the other side—meeting at different speeds because of
the parting it has suffered—tumbles among itself at the reunion
and creates a miniature Corrievreckan. We were doubtful
whether our craft could negotiate the place, and whether a
flood-tide would be the best condition for the attempt.

This was the problem we put to a crew of Clyde herring
fishermen whom we found by good fortune in the canal basin
(going south, the wise men!) and they waved the caution aside
with broad and reassuring gestures. 'Take it at the flood!' they
said it heartily, more than once, 'and one tide'll carry you right
to Oban.' This nautical wisdom was confident, and also welcome,
and we gladly laid aside our misgivings. It was now about three in
the afternoon, and a bonny blue-skied day, with the tide turning
in slack water, ready to flood.

The wind was southerly, looking as if it might remain steadily at our backs for the first time. So we stepped the masts again and rigged sail, looking forward to an effortless passage and a triumphant evening arrival in Oban, about thirty miles away. There was a launching scramble first among the low weedy rocks which the deep tide had left, and then we were away, paddling with the bows on the Dorus Mor, opening for us clear and inviting seven miles ahead.

Within half a mile out from the shore we could feel the insistent help of the wind almost behind us. It was a glorious moment as we shipped paddles, heaved up the sails by their paltry strings, and felt the sudden benevolent twitch as we went on steadily under sail. This was an interval for luxury, and we reclined at incredible ease in our cockpits, never dipping a paddle for the next mile or two, except for a momentary steering correction, while the canoes slid ahead with us at a good paddling pace. There was warmth at last in the sun, and it seemed truly as if our first stages might well prove to have been the worst.

Crinan was dwindling astern; the little bays of Kilmartin shore opened and closed on our right as we passed them; Craignish opened to the north, but its soft harbourage was not for us, and we knew it without regret. We scraped the little Island of Dogs, and felt ourselves to be on the actual threshold of the open sea. After the first well and surge of this sentiment we set to paddling, and pushed ourselves forward at what seemed to be the most perfect of all speeds, which is fast enough. The waves were growing now behind us, lifting us and running along beneath to escape from under the bows and leave us in a trough, which also travelled with us part of the way, until a new wave was elected to rise astern. We took to racing these wave children, going with them in little bursts, and laughing as they did. For this was innocent water. In the full opening of Loch Craignish we appeared to be hastening even more. Bigger waves now lifted us and carried us briefly, and although we did not guess the force of it then, the tide was urging us onward faster.

The doorway of the Dorus Mor was widening and nearing, with a black line like a step across the entrance. This line appeared at first to be merely our normal horizon, which was unusually limited because of the low level of the canoes. But as we approached, it did not appear to recede. Indeed, it thickened and rose markedly above the normal height of the horizon water all round—a phenomenon making for sudden unease. Our approach was swifter now, and, straining towards the forbidding dark barrier at the gap, our closer vision decomposed it into a sudden moving turbulence, as if mighty fish were distantly shoaling in the Dorus. From a mile off we could see the separate spouts and breakers which, in extreme miniature, would have been a sign of mackerel. As we peered and pondered, borne along, a lull in the wind sucked back to us the noise of a sea tumult.

We hauled down the sails and bundled them at the foot of the masts, slowing our speed. But by this time we were fairly in the race, and the noisy thresh of it filled all our hearing for the minutes that were to intervene before it cast us out beyond Craignish Point. The water changed in colour from a pleasant green to a sudden and sullen black, in which writhed streamers and trails of spent foam. And with the colour went the one-way rhythm of the water which had taken us here. The lifting waves that had followed and passed us in reliable attendance were drowned in a jauping popple. These separate wave-peaks reared individually and fell on us, punching at our sides and canvas tops, each one jerking us as solidly as a thrown bucket of stones.

'Keep paddling!' we shouted, although we had probably better have shipped paddles and given ourselves to the flood. Yet at that moment we had not realized that we were still travelling at full speed of the tide. Dipping paddles and tugging and staring at the near water, we appeared to be fixed and struggling in a static maelstrom. A glance farther ahead corrected the impression, for onwards, and approaching, was a low wall of water, higher than the level we were on, where the two irregular tide forces were heaving up the sea between them.

The wall seemed to dart and strike us, although it was we who rushed on it. Here the paddles felt new forces that made them kick in our grip as if hands in the water had seized to wrestle them from us. We were now in a moving group of whirlpools, and the noise was a hissing thunder. On the other side of our hulls of cloth and slats the sea gathered below our thighs like a horse bunching for the gallop. I struck the perimeter of a great swirl, swooped half round it and rammed Seumas with my point on his bow, remorselessly, although we were both striking fiercely apart. We clashed together for a moment along the length of the hulls, and parted on our ways again. Several times there would come a sudden subsidence of the near water, leaving one or other of the canoes sliding on the surface of a smooth bubble platform of sea, twenty yards across, pressed inches higher than the surrounding level like a lily-leaf adrift. Then this would burst and rip across and the spouts would storm at us, and a force below would seem to twitch the canoes deeply down below what buoyancy still ruled them.

By this time we had ceased to fight with our paddles, using them more as a balance against the rocking, which was too extreme to control. So, looking up, we had time to notice our onward progress, and to wonder why we still floated. As if to emphasize the movement, I was plucked round in a swirl like a giant circus roundabout, and found myself sweeping past the little cliffs of Craignish Point. They were only a few feet away, and they seemed to go past my face like the wall of a railway tunnel seen from a carriage window, the stuck limpets appearing like blurred white lines.

This was the last kick of the race, for here we burst through the narrowest neck of the channel and were disgorged into freer water, leaving the noise and threat of the Dorus Mor gradually behind us. There was still enough press in the flood to send us, spent and swirling, close up the rocks on the far side of Craignish. This entry we made to the Sound of Jura had surprise for at least one citizen on that sparse landscape. A kilted man was standing in a seaward-looking pose on the very point of the land—'Long Looking to Jura', as the Gaelic song says—when we came surging up on him from behind and were vomited out of the tide race almost at his feet. In the polite county of Argyll, it must have been shock, and no lack of grace, which made him unable to return our drenched salute. He stared and stared after us as we drifted out of his sight up the fringes of the Craignish rocks.

*from* QUEST BY CANOE

## F. FRASER DARLING

### THE SEALS ON TRESHNISH

· · \* · ·

THE good weather went out with August, for we woke to high wind and showers from the south-west on 1st September, the first day of what proved to be a trying fortnight. But we had come to watch seals and were full of eagerness and joy when the great beasts began to collect about the place in increasing numbers. There was one bull of tremendous size, probably nearly ten feet long and weighing, perhaps, several hundred pounds, who came to lie out at a particular place in the sound between Lunga and Creag a' Chaisteal. His personality soon became evident to us, and I think it was Dougal who christened him Old Tawny. What a magnificent head and proud bearing he had! Never since, either on the Treshnish or on North Rona, have I seen a bull seal to equal him in size or majesty.

His movements ashore were delightful to watch—the way he would make himself comfortable on the rock and then the expressive movements of his fore-limbs, which I prefer to call hands because they can be used in ways so like the human hand, fingers and knuckles as well, rather than as some awkward mittened limb of whale or manatee. You would see Old Tawny scratch his belly delicately with his finger nails, waft a fly from his nose, and then, half closing the hand, draw it down over his face and nose just as men often do. Then he would smooth his whiskers with the back of his hand, this side and that. His hands would be at rest over the expanse of his chest for a while, and then you might see him scratch one palm with the fingers of the other hand, or close his fist and scratch the back of it. A seal's movements are often a most laughable travesty of humanity, but considered more carefully as seal movements they have great beauty.

The wind increased to a gale from the south-west and we saw waves breaking three-quarters of the way up the face of Dun Cruit, or the Sanctuary Rock, which is one hundred and fifty feet high. Between there and Creag a' Chaisteal great rollers were coming in and breaking long before they reached the shore. The seals were out there obviously enjoying themselves. I saw Old Tawny letting the waves break on him and coming up again in the trough to wait for the next one. None of them was fishing; it was just the fun they were having.

The gale and rain seemed to reach a climax on the night of 4th September, and we had no sleep before 3.00 a.m. Then we went off oblivious to everything until six o'clock, when the wind had dropped and the rain stopped. Blessed peace. We turned over again, and the next thing we knew it was a quarter past nine. The seals were calling loudly in their high falsetto while we had breakfast, and I was thinking to myself that the tide should be low enough about noon to let us across to Creag a' Chaisteal. I looked over the cliff to see twelve cow seals lying out at Old Tawny's place. Soon there were sixteen, and then Old Tawny himself came out of the water and lay by them.

I had much to learn about the Atlantic grey seal at that time. This was the first time I had spent any considerable spell at one of their breeding grounds at the breeding season, and I was much afraid of being too eager to stalk them and frightening them away.

Money from scientific bodies and much goodwill from individual people had put me in this favoured position in which I could do a self-chosen job of work. Therefore, it was not for me to amuse myself with a very close stalk, if by that act I imperilled later research. My previous attempts at stalking seals at home and elsewhere had shown me that they were extremely wary. But as I looked at that mob of seals and Old Tawny, then at every inch of the ground between me and them, and felt the wind coming in from the west, I thought the job could be done. Surely a photograph of Old Tawny would justify my going.

Dougal and Alasdair wanted to explore part of Creag a' Chaisteal, so we three started together on condition they left the group of seals to me and kept well out of their sight and wind. We crawled over the floor of the sound on our bellies in full view of the seals two hundred and fifty yards away. But wind and sun were in our favour and we went extremely slowly over that expanse of tangle and wrack, myself encumbered with camera, lenses, and binoculars—nearly a hundred pounds worth of stuff about my neck. It was agonizing but exciting, and we got over and out of sight without arousing the suspicion of the seals.

Now I went on alone, a big stalk ahead of me and all over seaweed, or so I thought until I came to a place where I realized it would be better tactics to be in the water than to be in full view on top of a rock. I left my boots, stockings, binoculars and some of my camera gear, and waded in slowly until the water was nearly up to my middle. The bottom was so slippy and my tackle so precious. Then a cow seal came near to me in the water and was most interested in my slow and laboured progression. She was not frightened, just curious, and I changed the lens of my camera without mishap, took careful aim and got the photograph which later turned out to be a favourite. She was kind to me and went away quietly. Metaphorically, I raised my Sunday morning hat to the lady, for indeed it was the Sabbath, and then carried on.

I was over at last and crawling upon a sunken skerry, along the top of it and in full view of the seals at less than fifty yards range. By this time I was sweating and excited but had managed to keep my large red face to the ground. I took advantage of cover to shed more clothes and go forward with only the bare camera; then down the rock into some shallow water, moving so that it did not splash, crawling on again and then a peep to see where I was. Only twenty yards, but a rotten position for a photograph. On again with my face to the rock; foot after foot.

And now I was lying alongside Old Tawny, near enough to tickle him, and he was still dozing. I looked at the great furred belly of the seal, at his powerful hand with its five black claws. He rumbled inside and the very rock seemed to shake; never have I felt more insignificant. There is six feet three of me, but I was a dwarf beside him, and he was twice as high through the shoulder as I was, lying there beside him. I do not know how long I lay there in wonder at the beauty of the seal, but at last I brought myself to the serious and technical job of photography. The focusing, the exposure, the stops—and him. Was he in a good position? No, I was too near, his head was down and eyes closed.

I edged backwards, using only my body muscles, then I whistled gently and he raised his head to look about him. My chance had come and I took it—and it was the last exposure in the film of thirty-six!

Old Tawny looked round, laid his head down again for a moment and then up again. He looked at the recumbent figure beside him. It was strange; he had better get away from it, but he moved leisurely and without fright. If a human being can get close enough to a large animal, I find it will not take precipitate flight as it would if it saw him several yards away. I had got through the barrier of this beast's watchfulness and I should have had to make some positive movement to frighten him now. Luck was with me that day, the twelfth anniversary of my getting married, I noticed, and the portrait of Old Tawny is in my house, while Old Tawny himself, I hope, is still swimming the seas of the Treshnish Isles with his usual joy and serenity of carriage.

*from* ISLAND YEARS

# JOHN R. ALLAN

## THE CATTLE SHOW

· · ✻ · ·

THERE was a rising excitement about the morning of the show. The ploughmen appeared in their second-best—the tight trousers; the shapeless jackets of thick cloth like a pelt; the white shirt but no collar, each neckband being confined by a bright brass stud; and the new cap askew on the closely cropped hair. Even the cattleman, who lived in such close community with his beasts that the dung had dried on him, that one morning had used the scrubber and the dandy brush. At intervals, the slowest animals first, we set off to the show in the market town. Along the road we began to see our rivals, all the way being spaced by little flocks and herds and teams, with now and then a man riding a single mare or a crofter driving his only cow. People came out from houses and steadings to see us go by, sometimes with off-taking comments on our animals, sometimes with the long silent stare of those who live alone upon an island of distrust. So it went on till we came into the little town, where we had no time to think of anything but confusion and disaster. Every street converged its flocks and herds into the narrow lane leading to the showyard. By that time the animals had been excited. Chased by all the town dogs, harried by all the town children, shouted and sworn at by their drovers, they made sudden sallies into shops and gardens. At the head of the lane a few stewards tried to regulate the traffic, but they might as well have tried to regulate a herd of buffalo. All the beasts that had not been lost crowded past them, bellowing, baaing and slavering; dogs barked and sticks slapped over fat black quarters; the dung flew free and everybody shouted 'Hell.' When we got inside the showyard the confusion spread out as each drover tried to find his own and did find them and stalled or penned them in the appointed places.

When the clock struck eleven from the parish kirk, all the attendants doubled their efforts, making the sawdust fly like snow round the horses' feet. Spectators looked at their watches, then at the two tents, official and conniving under the elm tree. They saw a man with a very large badge in his lapel passing from the one to the other several times with bottles and glasses. It was a sign that the judges were being loaded and the battle would soon begin. Stewards, wearing badges of silver cardboard, ran about waving catalogues, calling on competitors to get ready, and urging the spectators towards the rings so that the animals might have room to move. After a monstrous deal of shouting, attention was fixed in the middle of the field. The judges came from beneath the elm tree in pairs. Sometimes there might be only one judge, but it was considered better there should be two, on the principle that two heads were better than one and each judge could keep an eye on the other. As they stepped into the ring I used to think they had awful majesty. They came from the distance. They were so famous you could sometimes read their names in the paper. And on that day, when the best of the countryside had been gathered together, they were the arbiters of judgment. They were, I thought, in a wonderful position and maybe they thought so too; for, although they were quite ordinary bodies, they took on a remote, impartial air for the occasion. During the next two hours their word was law, beyond all question.

Whatever the animals, the judging was a time of almost intolerable suspense; as a spectacle, the judging of the horses was supreme. Perhaps a dozen, or even twenty, mares would be led round the ring, first at a walk, and then at a trot. They frisked, they bounded, had moments of pretended fright and real panic in the walk while the attendants tried to make them hold up and show their points. But when the walk became a trot, the more rapid movement filled them with pride and joy. The great beasts, shining with health and care, pounded over the hollow turf, throwing back their hairy hooves till their bright shoes caught the sunlight. Strong and irresistible, necks arched, manes flowing, neighing, blowing out great cannonballs of breath, they carried their attendants along at the halter's end, as if it had been some old story of gods in animals' shape at sport with the sons of men. When the judges had seen enough of it they signalled that the animals be ranged before them, and somehow that was done, with the obviously good at one end and the obviously bad at the other. The judges proceeded with their priestly office. They ran their hands over the beasts, stood back with half-shut eyes, walked round, drew attention, shook their heads, agreed, moved one beast up a place and moved another down three. Meanwhile the spectators hung over the ropes, or leaned on their sticks if they were fat, important men, and all criticized the animals and the judges, at first with caution, but afterwards with feeling and force as the spirit kindled in them. Sometimes the judges took a long time to agree, and you could see emotion trying to win through on faces long schooled to express nothing but wary incomprehension. And when the decision was made, there was a surge of triumph and protest round the ring

and one mannie would cry, 'Dammit, the grey mare's got it.'
And his neighbour in disgust, 'Eh, dammit, aye.'

By one o'clock it was all decided and done with for another
year. Some had gotten red tickets and silver tickets to nail up in
the stable or byre. Some had gotten nothing but a deepened
sense of injustice. Most had just the feeling that it was dinnertime, that the refreshment tent was open, and they had all
afternoon before them.

The members of the Society dined in the hotel, where they all
sat down together along with the judges. The menu was simple,
traditional—cold salmon followed by cold roast beef; and, for
those who drank noxious liquors, a cup of coffee. Before the
dinner, and during it, the gentlemen had fortified themselves
against the speeches. So they returned to the field about a
quarter to three in an excellent good humour. The crowd was
now greatly increased, for the farmers' wives had come in, and
the young men and girls, and hundreds of town people. It was
now a purely social gathering where old friends met and old
sweethearts were reviewed. Through it all, those unfortunate
creatures who always get drunk at dinnertime on public occasions
weaved their uncertain courses round the fixed centre of the
refreshment tent, causing laughter, embarrassment and shame,
while their wives put a brave face on it, saying pleasantly, 'Oh,
come now, John,' and other wives thanked God their husbands
were not like that and never would be, at least until much later
in the day.

There was also a band, a good old-fashioned brass band in a
uniform, honest tradesmen of the cornet and bombardon. With a
lorry as a platform they took up their positions for offensive
action and began with one of those arrangements that were always
familiar but always somehow different. It was fine, virile stuff.
The big drummer made the drum go boom, cymbals clashed, the
bombardons grunted in a subterranean chorus, a man wrestled in
the coils of a flashing serpent from which he drew blasts of pain,

the trumpets affirmed the theme over and over again in brazen clangour, and the cornet, O sweet and heavenly horn, warbled above all a happy song of glee. How beautifully they sounded in the field, now borne towards us on the wind with a more than martial din, now carried away into the beechwood, thin and faint and far, like the horns of elfland calling among the rooks. Horses neighed, cows mooed, sheep and pigs called after their fashion—the music assumed all noises to itself. Even a shunting engine did no more than reinforce the man in the coils of the serpent. I'll never hear that sort of band again, good country tradesmen with their simple rhythm like the feet of horses on the road at night, for I'll never be the age again to enjoy an hour so much when all the senses are eager and the response immediate. It was all good—the heat of the day when the breezes failed, the smell of the trodden grass sharpened by herbs, the smell of dung and urine in the sun, the smell of the animals, the smell of food and beer from the refreshment tent, of whisky on men's breath and scent on women's sweat; everything—the attendants sitting beside their animals with sandwiches and beer, the old men that stood in twos and threes talking and listening absently as if the words did not much concern them; the drunks in all the stages through urgent friendship to collapse—everything, everything; and everything was wonderful. Not good. Not bad. There was no place for judgment. It was enough that so much existed. Wonderful there could be so much in the world and I in the middle of it.

from THE NORTH-EAST LOWLANDS OF SCOTLAND

## FOOTBALL IN GLASGOW

. . * . .

ASSOCIATION football is the overwhelming sporting interest of
Glasgow. It is sometimes said by the more foolish or perhaps by
the more snobbish Rugby enthusiasts that the great Soccer crowds
are mere masses of spectators watching paid performers but
taking no part in the game themselves. This is a false and shallow
judgment. The local passion is as much for playing football as for
watching it. There are schoolboys who get up at five of a summer's
morning to get in an hour of football before they set off on their
milk or newspaper rounds. The football pitches provided by the
schools and the Corporation are quite insufficient to meet the
immense demand. Each piece of waste ground is utilized, legally
or illegally. A rubber ball or even a rolled-up piece of paper will
do for a scratch game, with jackets for goalposts and perhaps a
police-watcher instead of a referee. If the majority of the spectators at the big matches do not play football regularly or in
regular teams, neither do the majority of the Rugby supporters.
Football under either code is a young man's game, but men who
could not possibly last a full soccer game on a full-sized pitch
snatch every chance to kick a ball around. The great crowds for
the great matches are composed of men who know the game
intimately because they played it hard and often so long as they
were able. They make immense noise and their arguments are
passionate and profane, but it is the violence of experts They
know what they are talking about, and they never indulge in the
merely ignorant clamour of a big boxing crowd.

The greatest occasion of the Soccer year is the International against England. When the match is played at Wembley, thousands take the train from Glasgow, armed with bottles and decorated with tartan scarves and tammies. They show perhaps rather too much of the Hogmanay spirit. The Londoners enjoy the colour, the pranks and the cheerful shouting, but they are hardly to be blamed if they are confirmed in their suspicion that a good many people in Glasgow drink a great deal too much. The invading Scots make a kind of proletarian Boat Race night out of the Wembley International. In essentials they may behave better than the Boat Race crowds but they certainly show the Londoners a more virile and violent conception of a good time than they are accustomed to. After the last International, I came back from Wembley by train. There was a Glasgow man keeping himself upright with much difficulty in the middle of the crowded compartment. It could justly be said that he was dressed for the part. In addition to the obligatory tartan scarf and tammy, he was wearing a kilt, with a whitewash brush for a sporran and a dustbin lid (City of Westminster) for a Highland targe. 'I'll no' be worth tuppence the nicht,' he said, with a beaming and confiding air. 'Tae tell you the truth, I'm no' worth fourpence the noo.' But, although the shades of mental night were closing in on him, he argued aggressively and persistently, with nobody replying, that the English had been supremely lucky to lose by only one goal, and that the Scottish eleven was individually superior in every position and even more heavily superior as a team.

His combative spirit was characteristic. The Glasgow man does not go to an International with any intention of distributing polite and impartial approval to both sides. He goes with the sole purpose of yelling himself into a frenzy in support of Scotland. The most brilliant demonstration of football skill gives him no satisfaction at all if Scotland fails to win.

His partisan passion is shown even more clearly when the match is played at Hampden Park, Glasgow. It has been said that the 'Hampden Roar' is worth a goal to the Scottish team. This is very likely untrue, but the Roar is nevertheless an intimidating and electrifying affair. There may have been something like it at the Fall of the Bastille, but there is nothing like it in any other sporting event in Britain. There is no malice behind the Roar, but only an ungovernable excitement and an intolerable anxiety that Scotland should win.

And yet, although the International draws the biggest crowd, it is not the most intense occasion of the football year. The clashes between Celtic and Rangers, the two leading Glasgow teams, rouse deeper and more dramatic passions, for these matches crystallize the racial and religious difficulties of Glasgow. The Battle of the Boyne, the Reformation, Irish Partition and all kinds of local rows and ructions play their part in inflaming feeling.

Celtic are identified with the Catholic interest and Rangers with the Orange. It makes no difference that some of the greatest Celtic heroes have been Protestants. These men are accepted as honorary Catholics, for football purposes, just as Mr. Attlee and Mr. Gaitskell are accepted as honorary toilers for political purposes. The identification may be arbitrary, but it is quite good enough for the faithful followers.

For many happy years, a Celtic versus Rangers match gave the highest degree of pleasurable excitement to everybody except the police. The shock troops on either side were organized in brake-clubs. A brake-club was a kind of Unfriendly Society of men who travelled to the match in their own hired bus. They wore tin helmets, club scarves and tammies and rosettes, and carried ricketties and banners and bugles, and sometimes a useful supply of rivets and pieces of paving-stone. Frequently battles broke out while the brake-clubs were converging on the football ground, until the police laid it down that the Celtic clubs must approach the ground from one end and the Rangers' clubs from the other. Next, the banners and ricketties were

forbidden, and all practical steps have been taken to put an end
to fighting, and stone and bottle throwing.

In days when feeling ran even higher than now, the frenzy of
the supporters found a readier echo in the field. Play was frequently described as 'robust', which meant that a fair shoulder
charge began with the heel of the boot and ended with the
back of the head. Every foul or alleged foul brought forth a cry
of execration,

> *'as if men fought upon the earth*
> *And fiends in upper air.'*

A bad (or inconveniently good) decision by the referee brought
a volley of outraged abuse and sometimes a volley of stones as
well. A goal for one side or the other was greeted by a triumphant bawling of 'Boyne Water' or 'Hail Glorious Saint Patrick'.
Such an atmosphere could not fail to have its effect on the players,
already excited by an exhausting and doubtful struggle. It is said
that during one particularly ferocious game, the Celtic captain
was exasperated when play was halted because of damage to the
ball. 'Never mind the ba',' he is alleged to have shouted, 'get
on wi' the gemme.' No doubt the story is an invention, but it has
symbolic value, and it is significant that the Celtic captain was a
Protestant.

The temperature of those invigorating contests is not quite so
high as it used to be, which is a loss to sporting excitement but a
gain to public order. Yet it remains true that the diehard supporter
of each side every Saturday gives his zealous support to his own
team and support no less zealous to the team which happens to be
playing the enemy. If the crowd at Celtic Park hear that Rangers
have gone down before Hearts or Dundee, they raise three
hearty though not particularly British cheers. Equally, Rangers
supporters take vast pleasure in the defeat of Celtic. Yet, on one
occasion, there was something like unanimity. That was on the
dramatic day when Rangers played Moscow Dynamo. The Dynamo

were a Communist team, and they were also a police team. The most fiery Celtic supporters agreed that, for this one day, they must wish well of Rangers. It took an immense moral effort to decide that there was something in the world more important than the local football feud, but the decision was made. All honour to these worthy men.

The players of the two teams are friendly off the field and in modern times they do not start a match with any prior intention of kicking each other around. There are still outbursts of violence on and off the field, but sometimes the teams will play each other for several games running with perfect sportsmanship and propriety.

And yet, the atmosphere of the Celtic-Rangers match is like no other. Stricter control and perhaps some softening of feeling have done a good deal to mitigate the violence, but the Celtic versus Rangers contest is still the most obvious indication of the social, racial and religious frictions and unresolved stresses of a city which has still something to learn in the way of tolerance. The contest takes the lid off The Problem.

*from* THE GLASGOW STORY

## ALASTAIR BORTHWICK

### HUNGER MARCH

· · * · ·

THE whole vast chain of the Black Cuillin, from Gars-bheinn to Sgurr nan Gillean, was stretched out like a curtain before us, with the sun, which had not yet dropped to our level, lighting the range from end to end. The mountains seemed close enough to touch. The morning mist was rising from them, softly, effortlessly, revealing first one buttress, then another, of the twenty peaks which stretched for miles, linked into a continuous whole by high ridges, scored by gullies, turreted, pinnacled, heaved up to the sky; rock, rock, and more rock as far as the eye could see. And, Black Cuillin or not, they were blue, the pale, delicate blue of a spring sunset, matt like a butterfly's wing. As the mist dissolved, more and more peaks took the skyline, more and more pinnacles broke the ridges, until only the gullies smoked. Then the last puff dissolved and broke, and they too were clear. The Cuillin were ours.

William began to sing. We slung on our rucksacks and plunged downhill to Camasunary.

We lay on an immense slab of rock, roasting in the sun, and trying to snatch some of the sleep we had lost on the previous night. The sun was pitiless. All morning the heat had grown; and now, at five o'clock in the afternoon when some respite might have been expected, it was worse than ever, for the sun was still high and the rock was releasing the stored heat of the day. Though, as Sandy pointed out, we were like four fried eggs in a pan, no escape was possible: at the place we had reached nothing grew. We were lost in a wilderness of bare rock which was hot to the touch.

William groaned at the casual mention of eggs. Eggs were a sore point. We did not talk about eggs. When we had reached Camasunary nine hours before in what we then imagined to be the last stages of hunger, we had found, not a village, but one house; and the owner of the house had not relieved our hunger by frying ham and eggs, for the very good reason that he was not at home and had locked the door behind him. We were, therefore, acutely conscious of the fact that our last real meal was thirty-three hours behind us, and our next one, to the best of our knowledge, thirteen miles ahead. We were lying on a wide terrace overlooking Loch Scavaig, hoping against hope that a small dot on the map, representing a spot three miles ahead, might be a house. Hoping was energy wasted. When we reached it, hours later, we found only scattered stones where a house had once stood. To eat, we had to reach Glenbrittle.

The view, from the point where we lay, was magnificent. Bare rock walls, on one of which we were perched, plunged down into Scavaig, a sea-loch. We were looking over and beyond it into the heart of the Cuillin horse-shoe, where naked cliffs sweep three thousand feet to the shores of Loch Coruisk, a fresh-water loch whose bed is far below the level of the sea. Still the butterfly blue dusted the rocks. There was no wind. Everything was calm, and vast, and still. And in the middle distance was a patch of gold and translucent green where the waters of Scavaig broke on a little beach. We looked at it. We looked at each other, and were unanimous. We should bathe.

But between us and the beach was the Bad Step, 'on which', says the Scottish Mountaineering Club's Guidebook to the Cuillin, 'there is not the slightest difficulty if crossed at the right place. Most people who get into trouble here attempt to cross too high up.' Perhaps we tried to cross too high up, perhaps we did hit off the proper route, but were too inexperienced, exhausted, and heavily laden for an easy passage to be possible. I do not know which of these alternatives is the true one, for in those days all of us had an exaggerated idea of the difficulty of the climbs we undertook, and none of us has seen the Bad Step since; but I do know that on that occasion the Bad Step lived up to its name.

To those who have confined their walking to England or the milder parts of the Highlands it may seem incredible that such a thing as the Bad Step can exist, for in these places there is never any natural difficulty which cannot be avoided without much trouble. If a boulder blocks the path, you walk round the boulder. If a river cannot be forded, you look for a bridge. But the Bad Step cannot be avoided: anyone following the south-west coast of Skye from Loch Slapin to Glenbrittle must cross it. The wide, easy terraces which make progress along the wall above Scavaig a simple matter are cut by a great rock buttress which falls straight into the sea from a point high on the cliffs. Like much of the rock in the district, it is black and utterly smooth in outline, so that it looks like an enormous whale with its tail in the water and its head far up the mountainside. Two parallel cracks slant across its back, about five feet apart, for twenty or thirty feet; and the only method we could devise, rightly or wrongly, for crossing it was to place our toes in the bottom crack and our fingers in the top crack, and shuffle. With forty-pound rucksacks dragging us outwards, this was exciting. Sandy was the only one to acquit himself well: he put on rubber-soled shoes and almost ran across it. I took twenty minutes. John and William gave it up altogether, toiled hundreds of feet up the mountainside, and crossed by a route which I suspect was considerably more difficult, thereby giving us the pleasure of watching them while we lolled at our ease, up to our necks in the sea, and jeering the while.

We slept a little after that, basking like seals in the golden bay, subconsciously delaying the evil moment when we should have to move again. I have never seen a more barren spot. We might have been on a volcanic island, upheaved from the Pacific, a thousand miles from anywhere, so naked and deserted was the picture of green sea, black rock, and the filigree of gold dividing them. Scavaig was remote from the world. It was good to lie there in the sun: lying still, one did not feel so hungry.

But by six o'clock some sense of responsibility had penetrated to our sun-drenched minds, and we realized that further delay would mean another night in the open. This was unthinkable. During the afternoon the way had been so rough and the sun so hot that we had stopped every ten minutes, and to avoid this we now fell back on the ancient army plan of walking for fifty minutes in each hour. How we came to believe that we should accomplish this over the abominable acreage of rock stretching before us it is difficult to understand: but believe it we did.

'Six-fifteen,' said Sandy with great conviction. 'Next stop seven-five.'

'Seven-five,' we said, and meant it.

Five minutes later, still overloaded with pride and fine intentions, we came upon the brambles, a great, tangled bed of them, rich and fat and purple, contriving somehow to draw life from this howling wilderness. And they were ripe. We wavered and halted, but did not dare to drop our rucksacks. Sandy looked at his watch as if to assure himself that fifty minutes had passed, and seemed surprised when he found they had not. We all stood looking at each other, and, casting sidelong glances at the brambles, attempted to stem sudden and overwhelming springs of saliva. Sandy cleared his throat nervously, and fiddled with a tie which was not there.

'Eh . . . forty-five minutes still to go,' he said miserably.

I made a shameless dive. The rest followed.

One hour later I drew away from the rest and sat down pensively by the edge of the loch, purple to the chin, feeling like the worst sort of Channel crossing, and certain that to my dying day I should never eat another bramble. Brambles are a snare and a delusion, drawing blood with their thorns and giving worse than nothing in return. Brambles are all pip and no nourishment. Taken in bulk, and we had eaten pounds, they settle in a cold mass and remain so, impervious to the digestive processes of man. The others joined me.

'We had to eat,' said John, 'but that was a mistake.'

We sat gloomily, spitting pips; and as we sat, the sun dropped below the horizon and we knew that we should not reach Glenbrittle that night. It was then that I discovered that I had dropped the tent-pegs as we crossed the Bad Step.

Hunger will lead one to desperate expedients, but we were not sufficiently desperate to touch the villainous brew which John graced with the name of breakfast. He had, he said, thought of it as he dropped off to sleep on the previous night. The problem was to render palatable our sole source of food, the bramble-patch beside the loch; and in an attempt to solve it he had boiled on a wood fire (the primus, he discovered, had no paraffin in it) half a pound of brambles. He had found the wood on the beach. The result was revolting, and reeked of smoke. Had there been sugar to flavour the mixture we might have overlooked its appearance; but without sugar that was impossible. It was of the consistency of lumpiness of the paste with which posters are stuck on hoardings, and was of a virulent purple which left the pot discoloured for weeks. I shook my head. I could not touch it. John ate one tentative spoonful and decided that the recipe was perhaps not such a good one after all. William embarked upon an elaborate discourse on the origins of Tyrian purple: the lost dye, he said, had no connection with boiled mussels as modern scientists claimed, but came from brambles gathered and boiled upon the beach of Scavaig. Sandy dumped the brew in the sea.

We were all hungrier than we had ever been in our lives; but we had slept well. Though the news that I had lost the tent-pegs had been greeted by groans, the accident was the best thing that could have happened, for it prevented us from erecting the tent.

Instead, we were forced to gather a pile of heather several feet deep and to spread the tent over it like a blanket. This bed, as well as being comfortable as a spring mattress, was really warm. Most of the cold in camp comes from below. The heather dealt so well with that, that the rug and tent were ample protection against the frosty night air. We slept in comfort for eight hours.

But hunger had become a serious problem. We had not eaten from plates for forty-eight hours, and even our miserable ration of sandwiches and chocolate was a memory of twenty-four hours ago. Glenbrittle was only eight miles away; but by this time we had no illusions about either the nature of the ground or of our own staying power. People have fasted for a month or more before now; but they have taken great care to do so at their ease, generally in glass cases at seaside resorts. They have not had to carry forty pounds over rough country with the temperature at seventy-five in the shade, a process which, we discovered, left the knees strangely weak.

The sun was as hot as ever. Any thought of walking for fifty minutes in each hour was unthinkable, for none of us could keep his feet for more than twenty minutes without a long rest, and this despite the change which had taken place in the outlook of the party. Until the previous night the journey had seemed to us a glorified picnic, lightly undertaken and lightly to be carried out. In our innocence, which did not admit of starvation in civilized Scotland, we had taken no precautions and made no plans, thought nothing of our inexperience and lack of condition, but had muddled happily along, secure in the belief that, however unfortunate the start had been, we should reach Glenbrittle and food that night. We had bathed and slept, admired the view, argued, stopped when we felt inclined. But now we had learned our lesson, which was that we could not take liberties with a wilderness. There was nothing of the picnic about that final day, but a slow, determined grind towards Glenbrittle. Hunger, we discovered, was not the localized pain we had imagined it to be. Once our stomachs had abandoned hope of attracting food by the conventional distress messages they were wont to send out three times a day, they ceased to be the seat of hunger. We were hungry all over. Our finger-tips were hungry.

By noon we were walking on heather, on the lip of the cliffs where the southern Cuillin drop into the sea. The sea was pale, transparent green, deep and abnormally clear. When we rested, we did so on the edge of the cliffs, and lay face-down, peering a hundred feet to the water and through it into green, silent, under-water Cuillin where fish swam. There were seals, too, barking where the Atlantic swell broke against the cliffs; and sea-birds flung themselves like white stones at the water and the fish below. Southwards were the Inner Isles, Rum, Eigg, Canna, fading into a blue haze.

Sandy was the first to drop out. We were five miles from Glenbrittle on a steady heart-breaking heather slope which dragged slowly to an upper moor. The slope was a mile long, and the heat was intense. Half-way up, Sandy dropped and refused to move.

'I just can't,' he said. 'I'm done. Leave me alone.'

We said we could not leave him there.

'It's all right,' he said; 'this will pass off. You carry on, and I'll follow when I'm able.'

No one was feeling particularly noble. We took him at his word, and left him. As it happened, it was the best thing we could have done, because my turn came next, and Sandy had reached me before I recovered. We carried on together, and a few minutes later we found William stretched out beside a burn. John, who held out until we reached the hostel, waited for us at the top of the rise, so that we finished together.

It was a curious experience, this feeling of weakness which suddenly took command of us. After more than two days of continuous heavy exercise, the brain and the body were functioning independently, so that the brain was left free while the body worked automatically. We were conscious, of course, that we were tired and hungry; but misery appeared to have reached a level just above that which the body could endure and below which it seemed impossible to go. There seemed no reason, we thought, why this state of affairs should not continue in the same dull rhythm of planting one foot before the other for the few miles which remained. Yet suddenly and conclusively, within the space of half an hour, three of us knew that we could go no farther until we had gathered strength. It was mental rather than physical, for the reactions of our bodies were numbed. Nor was it an ordinary rest. We just sat down, and, having sat down, knew we could not get up. Our legs refused to support us, and half an hour passed in each case before it was possible to go on. I remember thinking how odd it was, as I lay too weak to move, that I had £9 in my pocket. It seemed all wrong.

We had not seen a living soul for two days, and were only a mile or two short of Glenbrittle when we did. We had all recovered, and were resting on the moor below Coire Lagan, an immense rock amphitheatre which opens into the mountains above Loch Brittle. I was lying, gazing idly at Sgurr Alasdair, which is the highest mountain of the Cuillin, pure rock and immensely sharp, when I thought I saw something move. The sky was clear blue and cloudless, so that the final razor-edge of ridge below the summit was thrown up in sharp relief. And as I watched I saw four tiny figures crawl out on to the skyline and scramble slowly to the top. I was excited. I was tired, and thirsty, and hungry; but I still had it in me to be excited. We hoped to be up there soon.

Our imaginations broke all bounds on the final mile, and, nourished on starvation, reached heights of cruel and unwonted vividness. We thought of food so intensely that it seemed almost real. We took a delight in self-torture. Roast beef wrung my heart, roast beef slightly underdone, with Yorkshire pudding and thick gravy. The gravy, I insisted, must be thick, flowing round the rich brown flanks of roasted potatoes. What potatoes those were! They were real enough to touch, they and the French beans which lay beside them. Sandy swore he could smell the roast duck and green peas which filled his mind; and John was haunted by a complete seven-course dinner.

'My lords, ladies, and gentlemen,' he kept saying, 'dinner is served.'

We had not seen real food for nearly three days.

All this was rather pathetic, for our hopes exceeded our performance. We were too hungry to eat when we reached the hostel in the late evening. After a very moderate meal we tumbled into bed and slept for thirteen hours.

*from* ALWAYS A LITTLE FURTHER

# CLIFFORD HANLEY

## A BREATHLESS HUSH IN THE CLOSE TONIGHT

· · \* · ·

It is so ludicrous to imagine anybody actually building the things that I have always assumed that Glasgow's tenements have just always been there. Nobody could have put them up deliberately. When I first read about the ancient Picts running about in woad and scaring the life out of Caesar's legions, I took it for granted that they did their running about through the closes and back courts of Gallowgate where I was born.

The tenements are built extravagantly of good red sandstone, so that they have outlasted all those generations of Picts and are still there, and there doesn't seem anything anybody can do about them. It's true that in George Street and over in Govan, on the south side of the Clyde, some of them have started falling down spontaneously during the past ten years, but this is probably because people left them and they got lonely, and not through any constitutional weakness.

Most of them run to four storeys, built in rectangles to enclose the back courts. The back courts are divided by brick walls and brick-built wash-houses built for climbing over. It was on one of these that I made my first acquaintance with the terror that lurks in the big city. I would be four years old at the time, a perilous age in Glasgow because in order to live a full rich life at four, you have to attach yourself to the bigger fry and they can always run faster and jump higher than you can. So I was at the tail end of the line one night on the run along the top of the back court wall in Gallowgate and on to the high wash-houses of Cubie

Street, and I was good and far behind when I arrived at one of the obstacles of the course.

There was a turn in the wall, and in order to finish the run you had to dreep to the ground, stand on a dustbin to get astride the next bit of wall and then home to the roofs. The instant I lowered myself to dreep I knew it was too far. It was too dark to see the ground below, but I had heard enough about people breaking both legs. I had heard practically nothing else, in fact, from the time I could walk. But by this time I was hanging by my fingers and I couldn't climb back up either. I shouted, but nothing happened; so I screamed, and I had a good vibrant scream in those days. A Glasgow back court on a dark Tuesday night is the loneliest place in the world.

Some time later my sister Johanne, sitting in the house a hundred yards away and two storeys up, recognized the screams and bolted out to save me. She had to prise my fingers off the top of the wall before she could pick me down.

Danger and death were always familiar acquaintances. A few weeks later the boy downstairs, Tommy Mulholland, was playing on his rocking-horse on the first-floor landing when the whole thing overturned and carried him down a flight in a oner. It never seemed to cure him of riding facing the stairs, though it may seem odd that he was riding a rocking-horse on the landing at all.

The explanation is that the close in Glasgow is not just a hole in a building but a way of life. The close leads directly from the street to the back court, and the staircase to the flats above starts in the middle of it; and there is always something going on— somebody is always washing it or writing on the walls or hiding in it or giving a yell to test the echo.

After they wash it, the women give the stone flags a finish of wet pipeclay that dries bold and white and shows every footprint. Then, round the edges, they add a freehand border design drawn in pipeclay; sometimes a running loop like blanket-stitch, sometimes more tortuous key patterns, always mathematically accurate. . . .

Kicking other people's doors is a sport with its own added dimension when played in Glasgow's tenements. The gang requires an innocent sucker, and explains to him that it's his turn to be het, and that he must go to the top landing of the close and run down answering, 'It was me, it was me!' when he hears the question from the close. As soon as he gets up, the rest of the gang kick all the doors or ring all the doorbells on the lower landings so that the tenants will rush out in answer just as the victim passes with his innocent damning cry. I don't believe anybody was ever taken in with this. The victim always knew what the game was, but he played it out anyway.

We always talked about getting bits of rope and tying door-handles together in the closes or the landings so that two families would be trapped in their houses, but bits of rope were hard to find. Everybody remembered what a great game this had been the last time he played it, but nobody ever actually got a piece of rope *this* time. Except once. I was playing with two of the big yins, who let me come along to be het in the Singer's sewing machine game, and we actually got some string. I was given one end and they took the other, and we went into a close in Cubie Street to tie the two facing doors together. The two of them were giggling between themselves, and looking back years later I realized they were probably planning some surprise trick, like kicking their door and escaping in time to leave me behind and trapped. But as I stretched up to tie my end of string round my door-handle, the door casually opened and a man looked out. I was out of the close and scuttling for safety in less than a second, but the two others were caught red-handed.

*from* DANCING IN THE STREETS

---

# CONTEMPORARY PANORAMA

## FICTION

# ERIC LINKLATER

## THE DANCERS

. . * . .

*(The Pomfrets have mysteriously disappeared while celebrating Midsummer Eve on Eynhallow, a tiny uninhabited island in the Orkneys. The incident has occasioned much speculation and discussion.)*

THE young man with the stubbly beard sat still, staring at nothing with eyes that were alert and full of comprehension. He seemed to be listening to the throb of the steamer's screw and the answering wash of the sea. His lips moved slightly when a wave, louder than the others, ran with a slithering caress along the ship's side, and he smiled engagingly, looking at Mr. Pinto as though he expected an answering smile.

'The Möder Di,' (The Ninth Wave) he said, 'laughing at fishermen's wives. All summer she laughs lightly, but the laughter of her winter rut is like icebergs breaking.'

Mr. Pinto, remarking that it seemed to be a fine night, stepped out on to the deck.

'Oh, a glorious night,' said the young man with the beard, following him. 'Look at the clouds, like grey foxes running from the moon!'

'Indeed, there is one extraordinarily like a fox,' replied Mr. Pinto politely.

'She is hunting tonight,' said the young man. 'Foxes and grey wolves. And see, there's a stag in the west. A great night for hunting, and all the sky to run through.'

Mr. Pinto and his friend had the deck to themselves, and Mr.

Pinto began to feel curiously lonely in such strange company.

'Listen,' said the young man, pointing over the rail. 'Do you hear a shoal of herring talking out there? There's a hum of fear in the air. Perhaps a thresher-shark is coming through the Firth.'

Mr. Pinto, convinced that he had a lunatic to deal with, was considering an excuse for going below when the young man said: 'I saw you sitting silent while those fools were talking about Pomfret's disappearance. Why did you say nothing?'

'Because I didn't think any of their theories were good enough,' answered Mr. Pinto, feeling a little easier, 'and because I had no theory of my own to offer.'

'What do you think? You must think something?'

Mr. Pinto blinked once or twice, and then diffidently suggested, ' "There are more things in heaven and earth," you know; it sounds foolish, after having been quoted so often and so un-necessarily, but—'

'It does not sound foolish. Those others were fools. You, it seems, are not yet a fool; though you will be, if you live to grow old and yet not old enough. If you like, I will tell you what happened to George Pomfret and his friends. Sit there.'

Mr. Pinto, rather subdued, sat; and the young man walked once or twice up and down, his hair flying like a black banner in the wind, turned his face up to the moon to laugh loudly and melodiously, and suddenly said: 'They landed on Eynhallow in the quietness of a perfect evening. The tide was talking to the shore, telling it the story of the Seven Seals who went to Sule Skerry, but they could not hear it then. A redshank whistled "O Joy! look at them!" as they stepped ashore. But they did not know that either. They made a lot of noise as they walked up the shingle beach, and the rabbits in the grass, because they made a noise, were not frightened, but only ran a little away and turned to look at them.

'Mrs. Pomfret was not happy, but they let her sit on the rugs and she fell asleep. The others walked round the island—it is not big—and threw stones into the sea. The sea chuckled and threw more stones on to the beach; but they did not know that. And the sea woke birds who were roosting there, and the birds flew round and laughed at them. By and by the shadow of night came—it was not really night—and they sat down to eat. They ate for a long time, and woke Mrs. Pomfret, who said she could never eat out of doors, and so they let her sleep again. The others talked. They were happy, in a way, but what they talked was nonsense. Even Joan, who was in love, talked nonsense which she does not like to think about now.'

'Then—' Mr. Pinto excitedly tried to interrupt, but the young man went imperturbably on.

'Disney said one or two things about the birds which were true, but they did not listen to him. And by and by—the hours pass quickly on Midsummer night—it was time to dance. They had taken a gramophone with them, and Joan had found a wide circle of turf, as round as a penny and heavenly smooth, with a square rock beside it. They put the gramophone on the rock and played a fox-trot or some dance like that. Disney and Norah Disney danced together, and Joan danced with Samways. Two or three times they danced, and old Pomfret made jokes and put new records on.

'And then Joan said, "These aren't proper dances for Eynhallow and Midsummer Eve. I hate them." And she stopped the gramophone. She picked up the second album of records and looked for what she wanted; it was light enough to read the names if she held them close to her eyes. She soon found those she was looking for.'

The young man looked doubtfully at Mr. Pinto and asked, 'Do you know the music of Grieg?'

'A little of it,' said Mr. Pinto. 'He composed some Norwegian dances. One of them goes like this.' And he whistled a bar or two, tunefully enough.

The young man snapped his fingers joyously and stepped lightly with adept feet on the swaying deck.

'That is it,' he cried, and sang some strange-sounding words to the tune. 'But Grieg did not make it. He heard it between a pine-forest and the sea and cleverly wrote it down. But it was made hundreds of years ago, when all the earth went dancing, except the trees, and their roots took hold of great rocks and twined round the rocks so that they might not join the dance as they wished. For it was forbidden them, since they had to grow straight and tall that ships might be made out of them.'

The young man checked himself. 'I was telling you about the Pomfrets,' he said.

'Joan found these dances that she loved, and played first one and then the other. She made them all dance to the music, though they did not know what steps were in it, nor in what patterns they should move. But the tunes took them by the heels and they pranced and bowed and jumped, laughing all the time. Old Pomfret capered in the middle, kicking his legs, and twirling round like a top. And he laughed; how he laughed! And when he had done shaking with laughter he would start to dance again.

' "This is too good for Mother to miss," he said, "we must wake her and make her dance too." So they woke Mrs. Pomfret, and there being then six of them they made some kind of a figure and started to dance in earnest. Mrs. Pomfret, once she began, moved as lightly as any of them, except Joan, who was like thistle-down on the grass and moonlight on the edge of a cloud.

'And then, as the music went on, they found that they were dancing in the proper patterns, for they had partners who had come from nowhere, who led them first to the right and then to the left, up the middle and down the sides, bowing, and knocking their heels in the air. As the tune quickened they turned some-times head over heels, even Mrs. Pomfret, who held her sides and laughed to see old Pomfret twirling on one toe. And the gramophone never stopped, for a little brown man was sitting by it and now and again turning the handle, and singing loudly as he sat.

'So they danced while the sky became lighter and turned from grey to a shining colour like mackerel; and then little clouds like roses were thrown over the silver, and at last the sun himself, daffodil gold, all bright and new, shot up and sent the other colours packing.

'And everybody shouted and cheered like mad, and for a minute danced more wildly than ever, turning catherine-wheels, fast and faster in a circle, or shouting "Hey!" and "Ho!" and "Ahoi! Ahoi! A-hoi!"'

'Then they sank to the ground exhausted, and the Pomfrets looked at their partners who had come from nowhere; and were suddenly amazed.

' "Well, I'm damned!" said old Pomfret, and all the little brown men rolled on the grass and laughed as though they would burst.

' "Oh, they're the Wee Folk, the Peerie (Little) Men!" cried Joan delightedly, clapping her hands. "Peerie Men, Peerie Men, I've found you at last!"'

'And again the little men laughed and hugged themselves on the grass. By and by, still laughing, they drew together and talked among themselves very earnestly, and then the biggest of them, who was as tall as a man's leg to the mid-thigh, went forward, saying his name was Ferriostok, and made a little speech explaining how delighted they were to entertain such charming guests on Eynhallow; and would they please come in for break-fast?

'Some pushed aside the stone on which the gramophone had been standing and, as though it were the most natural thing in the world, the Pomfrets went down rock stairs to a long, sandy hall, lit greenly by the sea, and full, at that time, of the morning song of the North Tide of Eynhallow. They sat down, talking with their hosts, and then two very old little men brought stone cups full of yellow liquor that smelt like honey and the first wind after frost. They tasted it, curiously, and old Pomfret—he was a brewer, you know—went red all over and said loudly, "I'll give every penny I have in the world for the recipe!" For he guessed what it was.

'And the little men laughed louder than ever, and filled his cup again. One said, "The Great King offered us Almain for it eleven hundred years ago. We gave him one cup for love, and no more. But you, who have brought that music with you, are free to our cellar. Stay and drink with us, and tonight we shall dance again."

'No one of them had any thought of going, for it was heather ale they drank. Heather ale! And the last man who tasted it was Thomas of Ercildoune. It was for heather ale that the Romans came to Britain, having heard of it in Gaul, and they pushed northwards to Mount Graupius in search of the secret. But they never found it. And now old Pomfret was swilling it, his cheeks like rubies, because Joan had brought back to the Peerie Men the music they had lost six hundred years before, when their oldest minstrel died of a mad otter's bite.

'Disney was talking to an old grey seal at the sea-door, hearing new tales of the German war, and Joan was listening to the Reykjavik story of the Solan Geese which three little men told her all together, so excited they were by her beauty and by the music she had brought them. At night they danced again, and Joan learnt the Weaving of the Red Ware, the dance that the red shore-seaweed makes for full-moon tides. The Peerie Men played on fiddles cut out of old tree-roots, with strings of rabbit-gut, and they had drums made of shells and rabbit-skins scraped as thin as tissue with stone knives. They hunt quietly, and that is why the rabbits are frightened of silence, but were not afraid of the Pomfrets, who made a noise when they walked. The Peerie Men's music was thin and tinkly, though the tunes were as strong and sweet as the heather ale itself, and always they turned again to the gramophone which Joan had brought, and danced as madly as peewits in April, leaping like winter spray, and clapping their heels high in the air. They danced the Merry Men of Mey and the slow sad dance of Lofoden, so that everybody wept a little. And then they drank more ale and laughed again, and as the sun came up they danced the Herring Dance, weaving through and through so fast that the eye could not follow them.

'Now this was the third sunrise since the Pomfrets had gone to the island, for the first day and the second night and the second day had passed like one morning in the sandy hall of the Little Men; so many things were there to hear, and such good jokes an old crab made, and so shockingly attractive was a mermaid story that the afternoon tide told. Even the sand had a story, but it was so old that the Peerie Men themselves could not understand it, for it began in darkness and finished under a green haze of ice. And since the Pomfrets were so busy there they heard no sound of the chauffeur's visit and the Peerie Men said nothing of it. They had taken below all the rugs and cushions and hampers and gramophone records, and brushed the grass straight, so that no trace was left of the Midsummer dancing—except the tag of Joan's stocking suspender, which was overlooked, so it seems.

'The old grey seal told them, in the days that followed, of all that was going on by land, and even Mrs. Pomfret laughed to hear of the bustle and stir they had created. There was no need, the Peerie Men found, to make them hide when more searchers came, for none of the Pomfrets had any wish to be found. Disney said he was learning something about the sea for the first time in his life (and he had followed the sea all his life), and Norah sang Iceland cradle-songs all day. Old Pomfret swilled his ale, glowing like a ruby in the green cave, and Joan—Joan was the Queen of the Peerie Men, and the fosterling of the old grumbling sand, and the friend of every fish that passed by the sea-door. And at night they danced, to the music of tree-root fiddles and pink shell-drums, and above all to that music which you think was made by Grieg. They danced, I tell you! . . .'

The young man tossed up his arms and touched his fingers above his head; he placed the flat of his foot on the calf of the other leg; twirled rapidly on his toes. 'Danced, I say! Is there anything in the world but dancing?' And he clapped his heels together, high in the air, first to one side and then to the other, singing something fast and rhythmic and melodious.

Mr. Pinto coughed nervously—he was feeling cold—and said: 'That is an extraordinarily interesting story. But, if you will pardon my curiosity, do you mind telling me what reason you have for thinking that this actually happened to Mr. Pomfret and his friends?'

'Reason!' said the young man, staring at him. His hair blew out on the wind like a black banner, and he laughed loudly and melodiously.

'This reason,' he said, 'that I am Otto Samways!' And he turned, very neatly, a standing somersault on the deck and came up laughing.

'They sent me away to buy something,' he said, 'and when I have bought it I am going back to Eynhallow to dance the Merry Men, and the Herring Dance, and the Sea Moon's Dance with Joan.'

And once again he sang, very melodiously, and turned a rapid series of catherine-wheels along the deck.

'To buy what?' shouted Mr. Pinto, as he disappeared.

'Gramophone needles!' bellowed the young man, laughing uproariously.

# GUY McCRONE

## THE ARISTOCRAT

· · * · ·

THE day of rejoicing was hot. Sir Charles had spent an anxious week, looking a hundred times a day from the windows of Duntrafford at threatening clouds or actually falling rain. But suddenly on Saturday morning the old man, as he sat up in bed breakfasting, saw that the weather had cleared, and that a hot June sun already high in the summer heavens was causing a steamy mist to rise from the parklands beyond the lawn, and was beginning to dry the sodden canvas of the great marquee. This was better. Sir Charles ordered his man to fetch him the tussore suit he had worn when he was in India, chose a bright tie, and put them on with much satisfaction. His lady, wearing black spotted foulard and a large leghorn hat, wagged her ebony stick at him and went off into peals of eldritch laughter. Her husband merely growled, muttered something about her not being fit to have a grandchild, and marched out of the house to inspect the preparations, heedless of her cries that he should remember that the grass must still be very wet.

The morning was delicious. In the late Ayrshire June the spring still lingered. The foliage had become rich and deep, but it had not yet taken to itself the dark, glossy green of midsummer. Followed by his two old house spaniels, Sir Charles, his hands clasped behind his back, stumped about enjoying himself. Trestle-tables were being set up in the marquee by caterers' men. He told them that he thought it was ridiculous to be arranging them in this way; that they should be arranging them in that other way; then walked off, feeling he had shown these fellows who was in authority.

At the finely-wrought iron gates of his walled garden, he commanded his spaniels to sit and wait for him, peering back through the ornamental tracery at two despondent pairs of blood-shot eyes that looked up as though they had been excluded from Paradise; told them to be good doggies, and went on down the damp, scented turf alleys to see that his gardeners had carried out his instructions. Even Sir Charles had little to complain of. This Ayrshire garden was a miracle of luxuriance refreshed. The herbaceous borders were lavishly splashing their colours against the sombre green of the old yew-trees. Early roses, the raindrops still upon them, were sparkling in the sun. Tubs of geraniums and hydrangeas had been brought out from under glass and set about to add to the riot. Fruit was beginning to shape itself on the apple-trees, trained against the south wall. Sir Charles went, exchanging greetings with his gardeners, examining the trimmed edges, and pulling up the odd weed that seems to appear from nowhere after a warm, wet night. With a parting word that the men had better keep their eyes open while the mob walked round this afternoon, he turned and left the garden.

At a distance he could see that luncheon guests were beginning to arrive: Mungo's relatives from Glasgow, probably. This was annoying. Was it that time already? He had meant to go round and say good morning to his grandson, and ask his daughter Margaret how she did. But now those Moorhouse women would be gibbering and swarming all over the place, and making a fuss over a baby who meant nothing much to them. There they were, all silks and feathers and parasols, emptying themselves out of the wagonette and chattering like magpies. His wife and son-in-law were dealing with them. Well, let them. He would see them all at lunch. Sir Charles stalked round a rhododendron bush in full bloom, hurried down a path in the shrubbery and entered the house by the side-door.

He found his butler in the pantry, and told him to bring a glass of madeira to his dressing-room, the only place where, today, his privacy was secure against invasion. He sat down in an easy-chair before the empty fireplace, sipping his wine and resting. He felt a little tired. After all, a man couldn't stay young for ever. But his wine was doing him good. Giving him heart. Making him feel that life had treated him well. There had been Charlie's death, of course. But on this radiant day that belonged to his grandson, he mustn't feel bitter, even about Charlie. He rose, went to a drawer in his desk, took out a little daguerreotype photograph of his son, and sat down again to examine it. Charlie . . . Margaret, good girl, had just been doing everything that could be done to staunch that wound.

He still had half his wine to finish. It was comfortable and pleasant here. The warm scents of June were coming in through the open window; perhaps, if he closed his eyes for a little. . . .

Lunch was announced, and after some waiting Lady Ruanthorpe came to look for him. She found him sleeping in his chair.

'Charles! Wake up! We had no idea where you had got to.'

He opened his eyes slowly.

'What's that on the floor?' She saw that a little gilt square was lying at his feet, half hidden in the bearskin rug. She bent down, picked up the picture of her son, fumbled for her glasses and examined it silently for a time; then put it back in its drawer.

'Hurry, Charles,' was all she said. 'You're keeping everybody waiting.'

*from* WAX FRUIT

# JANE H. FINDLATER

## THE LITTLE TINKER

. . * . .

THE little tinker was wakening to his fifth morning in the world, when a slow procession came winding up the long hill road that leads to the Glen Farm.

All the Reids; Richard carrying the tent sticks; Rab slouching along, his dilapidated pipes under his arm; Jock the tinsmith with the instruments of his trade. Their wives were heavily burdened; for each had a baby tied upon her back, and carried, moreover, a load of tin cans, 'nawken's chaeterie', as they called them, for sale on the road. The older children followed at their own sweet will, the younger ones packed into the donkey-cart which in general ended the procession. But this morning the Reid forces seemed to have been augmented; for a second little cart, led by two more men, came after the other.

Jockie and Gib scoured ahead to the farm and burst into the byre to impart a great bit of news to their mother. 'Grannie's on the road, Mither!' they screamed; and again, 'Grannie's on the road! She's oot-bye!'

At the sound of these words Mary sat up upon her elbow, as if the news startled her. An expression very like fear crossed her face. She hugged the little tinker closer against her side.

Looking out from the darkness of the byre into the morning light she could see the whole procession of men and women framed like a picture by the doorway, as they came trailing towards the farm. When they reached the gate the procession halted, and two of the men lifted out of the second donkey-cart the strangest object imaginable.

Seated in a large creel of plaited willows, much in the attitude of a Buddha, was an old woman. So old she was that Time seemed to have done with her—had given her up apparently as a bad job, and decided to let her choose her own date for death. Not a tooth was left in her head, and her hands were shrivelled away till they resembled the claws of some ancient bird. All appearance of life had long ago left the flesh of her face—it was exactly like that of a mummy; but deep in their sockets her bright blue eyes flashed with a strange vindictive gleam like the eyes of a ferret.

This weird relic of humanity had indeed trodden the earth for the extraordinary period of a hundred and four years. The tribe held her sacred, they obeyed her every nod, would almost have worshipped her, and trembled before her displeasure, for she was believed to have uncanny powers. A glance of those terrible old blue eyes could, it was thought, 'owerlook' anyone who displeased her. She had never slept under a roof in all her hundred years. On the ground she had lain, and would lie till that time, surely not to be long delayed now, when it would be her bed for ever. Of all the sons and daughters she had borne, not one now survived. Long years ago she had seen her children's children die—yet here she was still. There is something that chills the blood in such permanence of the impermanent. It seems to shut out the survivor from the great human family whose members are linked together by the common tie of mortality.

This old woman was a tremendous asset to the Reid tribe, for her uncanny appearance and almost fabulous age made the country-people hold her in great awe. There was not a farmer's or shepherd's wife in the district who would have dared to refuse Grannie Reid an alms. She had been 'on the road' so long before their day—so long before their father's or grandfather's day! At the Glen Farm, where Macphersons had lived for three generations, they had a tradition that the present Macpherson's grandfather remembered Grannie a hearty woman in his boyhood.

At some far-off date in their tribal history, the Reids had divided into two bands. One migrated to Argyllshire, while the other remained in the old Perthshire haunts. Then a fierce dispute arose between them for the possession of Grannie. Long and heated was the contest, till at last they came to a compromise; she was to be a joint possession, sometimes in charge of one branch of the family, sometimes of the other. They did not pretend to love her; but they feared her exceedingly, and there was abundance in the camp when Grannie was with them.

The old creature was despotic to a degree. She migrated from district to district, from county to county, as the fancy took her, seated in her creel in the little cuddy-cart, and waited on with servility by her many descendants. In this way she made dramatic appearances from time to time among her kindred. Suddenly, perhaps, as they crouched round the camp fire late at night, the rattle of the cuddy-cart would sound, and in the cart was the creel with the dread little figure of Grannie squatting in it as upright as if she were carved out of stone. . . . Then came a stir among them all, for Grannie demanded the best of everything— the most sheltered corner of the ragged tent, the tastiest bone to pick.

The children fled before the old woman in terror, disappearing at sight of her as rabbits whisk into their holes at sight of a dog.

The day after her arrival in a place, Grannie would set off to 'work' in the neighbourhood. Her methods were very simple, but quite effective.

The cart stopped at the door of the house she desired to visit, and the two Reids who were deputed to carry the creel of the old despot lifted it out of the cart. They never knocked at any door, simply lifted the latch and walked into the house. There they deposited Grannie's creel, right in the middle of the floor; and there she sat, glinting out of her wicked old eyes at the frightened women and children who hastened to do her bidding. Tea, tobacco, potatoes, old clothes she would demand—and she generally got whatever she asked. Her bearers in the meantime stood by the door, waiting the signal to lift the creel and carry it out again. Thus the old creature went on from house to house, in a kind of royal progress, till she extracted as much as she required in the way of food and clothing.

But this morning Grannie Reid had not come upon a begging expedition to the Glen Farm—she had come in quest of her erring great-great-granddaughter-in-law. For, on arrival at the camp the night before, Grannie had been met by the news of the little tinker's birth and the rumour of his proposed adoption. Here indeed was matter for prompt interference.

Having discovered where Mary was housed, Grannie directed the bearers to carry the creel into the byre, that she might come face to face with the culprit. At sight of her ancient relative Mary sat up on her bracken couch, clasping the baby tightly in her arms, but spoke not a word. There was an oppressive silence for a minute; then the vials of Grannie's wrath were poured out:

'Sae it's a fine leddy we've got here!' she said with biting sarcasm—'a braw leddy!—maybe ye'll spare an auld body a puckle tea, mem?—me that's been sleepin' out-bye a' this coorse weather, an' you sae warm and dry?'

Mary winced, but was not quick-witted enough to find any retort to make. She kept silence, rocking the child in her arms and pretending to be very busy with him.

'D'ye no' think shame tae be lying there an' the bairn fower days auld?' the old woman asked next, in a contemptuous tone; and at this taunt poor Mary faltered out the tale of her illness and sufferings in the storm. But it did not touch Grannie one whit. She only despised Mary from the bottom of her heart, and thought her a hopeless degenerate.

'An' ye're tae mak' a gadgie (house-dweller) o' the bairn, they're tellin' me!' she said. 'He'll be as fine as yersel, then!'

'Weel, Grannie, the leddy says she'll gie him schoolin' an'

mak' a braw man o' him, an' he'll hae siller o' his ain afore he's twenty,' Mary pled.

'Schoolin'!' the old woman screamed—'Schoolin'?—wha wants schoolin'? A pretty like nawken (tinker) he'll be wi' schoolin'! Did ye ever hear tell o' a nawken could read or write?'

Then Mary, with sudden injudicious frankness, expressed her secret.

'Eh! but I'm no' wantin' the laddie to be a nawken. It's a gey hard life, Grannie.'

Here was open rebellion against the established order of things; and having once uttered her rebel thought Mary faced the old tyrant bravely, laying before her all Miss Nellie's schemes for the future of the child. No homeless wanderer was her little tinker to be in years to come, but a rich man with house and land of his own somewhere across the sea ('t'ither Watches', as Mary expressed it in tinker talk). In this wonderful country men could always make gold, and her son would found there a new race of Reids richer and happier than his fathers.

All this poor Mary expressed, oh! so falteringly and haltingly; for she was afraid of Grannie, not very sure of the scheme herself, but anxious, somewhere in the depth of her darkly ignorant mind, to do something for the child. She had, however, to reckon with one of the most immovable things in human nature the intense conservatism of extreme old age. For, like a pool of water slowly congealing on a bitter night, the heart of man is apt to contract, with the passing of time, into a terrible immobility.

When, exhausted by her eloquence, Mary sank back against the pillow, the old woman burst out into a torrent of bitter protest.

Her tinker talk, framed partly of Scotch dialect, partly of cant words, would need a philologist to do it full justice.

'A braw bodachan (man) ye'll mak' o' the bairn gin ye gie him ower tae gadgies!' she cried; and then she came to the gist of the argument—her deep contempt for these same 'gadgies'—this whole race of pitiful house-dwellers. They were afraid of everything; afraid of cold and heat; of wind and rain; of hunger and thirst. Was there a gadgie among them who would dare to sleep on the lennam (ground) on a winter night? She sat there, this strange survival, and discoursed on the supreme advantages of the tinker mode of life as compared with that of the house-dweller, much as an ancient oak tree endowed with speech might discourse to the saplings of the wood upon the restrictions of a hot-house existence.

'Hae I no' had my health a' my hunner years?' she asked triumphantly; 'an' did ever I sleep in a wuddrus (bed)? There wasna ane o' my bairns born in a keir (house), an' I had twal' o' them. . . .' She paused, searching back in the recesses of memory. Scenes a-many of birth and of death alike surged up from the past and moved before her mind's eye. Munching her toothless jaws as if she chewed something tangible in these memories, the old woman sat in silence for a minute, then recommenced her tale:

'Aye! . . . twal' . . . eicht sons an' fower dachters . . . an' a' in the grave lang, lang syne! . . .'

She paused to ruminate again, before she added, 'But mind, the nawken manishies (tinker women) hae their weans easier: thae gadgie wives make an unco' work aboot haein' a bairn. Mony's the time I've seen me tak' the road again wi' my bairn on my back an' it no' two oors auld. . . .' At this hardy reminiscence Mary winced again, ashamed of her own softness. This was exactly what Grannie desired; she watched the effect of her words, and then went on to impress her lesson if possible more deeply:

'The same wi' death—they get awa' easier. Ye'll no' mind my son Richard—ech! no—he was deid fifty years syne. . . . Weel, Richard had a hoast, syne a doctor body doon Aberfeldy

way cam' roond by the wattles (tents) an' said it was sinfu'
keepin' a deein' man oot-bye in the cauld. Syne they pit him
intil a granzie (barn), puir man. . . . A sair time he had o't—he
couldna get awa'.'

The old woman paused significantly, then nodded her little
withered head, and smiled a cunning, cunning smile. 'But I
helpit the puir lad: "Bing Avree, (come away, Richard),'' says I
intil his lug; "D'ye no jan it's morgan? (Do you not know it's
morning?),'' an' wi' that he up an' oot frae the granzie . . . a
shuker rattie it was (a clear moonlight night it was). I laid him
doon oot-bye on the lennam, an' he hadna ta'en three breiths o'
the caller air afore he got awa'. . . .'

Mary gasped at this horrible reminiscence and hugged the baby
to her heart, much as the father in the song clasps his son when
the Erl-King whispers in his ear: could it be that she would ever
thus wish to hasten the departure of the little creature whom she
had endowed with life? She did not, of course, express the
thought in these grandiloquent words; but it darted through
her mind in some sort of form, and she shuddered.

'Aweel, Mary,' the old woman said, 'tak' yer way o't—mak' a
gadgie o' the bairn if ye please—it's truth I've telt t'ye.'

With these parting words, the old woman beckoned to the
lads who had carried her in. At her signal they slouched forward
and lifted the creel again. Mary was forced to speak.

'Are ye for the road then, Grannie?' she asked timidly.

'Syet (Yes),' Grannie answered laconically, without even
turning her head in Mary's direction.

'Ye've no' seen the bairn,' Mary cried, distress in her voice.

'Ugh! I'm no' carin' for gadgie bairns,' the old woman
retorted—she would not evince the slightest interest in this
unworthy offshoot of her tribe. Her bearers hoisted the creel
between them and started for the road again. Mary gazed after
their retreating figures as they marched across the yard and
through the gate, carrying their curious burden.

Down on the road below the farm the whole good-for-nothing cavalcade of the Reids was to be seen, halted by the dyke-side. The very air reeked of them; an indescribable rank smell of wood-smoke, old rags, and filth. Mary's husband was there, but he did not even trouble to saunter up to the farm to see his new-born son.

As Mary gazed out at her tribe she gave a deep sigh; 'Aweel!' she said aloud to herself, and again, 'Aweel!' as if she was renouncing something. A few minutes later the cavalcade moved on. Jockie and Gib, however, rushed up to the byre with a parting message to their mother:

'Faither says ye may gie the bairn tae the leddy for a rij (sovereign) an' we're aff Aberfeldy wye.'

Having delivered this fond paternal message, the children darted off to the farm to beg a last scone from Mrs. Macpherson before they took the road.

Here was a dilemma for poor Mary—her husband evidently wanted his money, and yet Grannie was bitterly opposed to the child's adoption. Mary knew well enough that she, not Jock, would get the blame and would come under Grannie's ban. Grannie seldom found fault with the men—they were sacred in her eyes; she reserved all her wrath for their unfortunate wives. If Jock was 'angered' by not getting the money as he expected, he would probably beat her; but Mary had often been beaten. She could face the thought of that better than the fear of Grannie's tongue, and (oh, horrible over-mastering terror!)—the idea that she and the child might be 'overlooked' by the old woman. Mary was not accustomed to doing much thinking; to and fro in the darkness of her untutored mind she tumbled the arguments for and against the scheme till she was confused and weary. She would give the child to the lady—she would not give him; Jock wanted the money—Grannie would be 'angered'; she herself wanted to keep the child—yet equally she wanted him to be given this wonderful chance that had come his way so un-

expectedly. There seemed to be no light anywhere on the
path. . . .

In the evening when Mrs. Macpherson came into the byre she
thought that her patient was very restless.

'What ails ye, Mary? Are ye not feeling so well?' she asked
kindly.

Mary only shook her head.

'Ye'll soon be getting up,' Mrs. Macpherson went on, anxious
to cheer her; 'you're that strong and healthy it's wonderfu'.'

'Aye,' Mary assented, and added with a shy impulsiveness,
'Ye've been gey kind, mistress.'

'I'd do as much for any sick pairson,' said Mrs. Macpherson;
she had a touch of self-righteousness in her nature which made it
a great pleasure to her to make this announcement. Certain
texts of Scripture crossed her memory at this moment, and gave
her a feeling of virtuous satisfaction: 'Do good unto all men,' she
found herself quoting, and then was pulled up by the remainder
of the text, 'especially those that are of the household of faith.'
She could not in the wildest way connect poor Mary with the
household of faith; so she was robbed of any satisfaction in that
text, and had to fall back upon some of the other exhortations
to good works which seemed more applicable.

'Well, good night to ye, Mary,' she said. 'If ye get a good
sleep ye'll be all right the morn.'

'Aye, mistress, I'll be fine,' Mary replied.

The next morning, just as dawn broke in the east, Mary rose
from her bracken bed and opened a chink of the byre door. The
bitter wind blew in, but she did not seem to notice it. No light
shone there yet, and there was no sound anywhere except the
whistling wind as it blew round the corners of the house. . . .

Mary shut the door again, and felt her way back to the bed.
On the box beside it Mrs. Macpherson had put a candle and a
box of matches—not without misgivings lest Mary should burn
down the byre some night. Great admonitions had been given her

on the subject, so that she scarcely dared to light the candle. But this morning it was lighted, and by its feeble guttering flame Mary began to dress. All her poor garments had been dried for her, and they lay beside the bed. One by one she put them on, slowly, almost regretfully it seemed. She then flung her old green tartan shawl over her shoulders and in its folds she deposited the little tinker. With a sigh she stood and looked round the barn. . . . So might a king renounce his kingdom.

Last of all, Mary lifted the great bundle of tin cans she had carried on the night of her arrival, and swung them over her arm. She was ready for the road once more.

Then, as if a sudden thought had struck her, she stopped and detached a large tin pail from the bundle. It was all she could offer to Mrs. Macpherson in recognition of her kindness.

She laid it on the doorstone of the byre where it must be found, then turned away resolutely and trudged off through the darkness with her long swinging step. The little tinker did not like the cold wind; he buried his tiny head deep in the folds of the tartan shawl and gave a shrill whimpering cry.

He seemed to be entering a protest against this decision which pledged him for ever to the life of his fathers.

*from* THE LITTLE TINKER

## LEWIS GRASSIC GIBBON

### THE THUNDERSTORM

. . * . .

IT was then, in a lull of the swishing, she heard the great crack of thunder that opened the worst storm that had struck the Howe in years. It was far up, she thought, and yet so close Blawearie's stones seemed falling about her ears she half-scrambled erect.

Outside the night flashed, flashed and flashed, she saw Kinraddie lighted up and fearful, then it was dark again, but not quiet. In the sky outside a great beast moved and purred and scrabbled, and then suddenly it opened its mouth again and again there was the roar and the flash of its claws, tearing at the earth, it seemed neither house nor hall could escape. The rain had died away, it was listening—quiet in the next lull, and then Chris heard her Auntie crying to her *Are you all right Chrissie?* and cried back she was fine. Funny, Uncle Tam had cried never a word, maybe he was still in the sulks, he'd plumped head-first in when he'd heard of the old woman that Semple was sending to help keep house in Blawearie. They were off to Auchterless the morn, and oh! she'd be glad to see them go, she'd enough to do and to think without fighting relations.

The thunder clamoured again, and then she suddenly sat shivering, remembering something—Clyde and old Bob and Bess, all three of them were out in the ley field there, they weren't taken in till late in the year. Round the ley field was barbed wire, almost new, that father had put up in the Spring, folk said it was awful for drawing the lightning, maybe it had drawn it already.

She was out of bed in the next flash, it was a ground flash, it hung and it seemed to wait, sizzling, outside the window as she pulled on stockings and vest and knickers and ran to the door and cried up *Uncle Tam, Uncle Tam, we must take in the horses!*

He didn't hear, she waited, the house shook and dirled in another great flash, then Auntie was crying something, Chris stood as if she couldn't believe her own ears. Uncle Tam was feared at the lightning, he wouldn't go out, she herself had best go back to her bed and wait for the morning.

She didn't wait to hear more than that, but ran to the kitchen and groped about for the box of matches and lighted the little lamp, it with the glass bowl, and then found the littlest lantern and lighted that, though her fingers shook and she almost dropped the funnel. Then she found old shoes and a raincoat, it had been father's and came near to her ankles, and she caught up the lamp and opened the kitchen door and closed it quick behind her just as the sky banged again and a flare of sheet lightning came flowing down the hill-side, frothing like the incoming tide at Dunnottar. It dried up, leaving her blinded, her eyes ached and she almost dropped the lantern again.

In the byre the kye were lowing fit to raise the roof, even the stirks were up and stamping about in their stalls. But they were safe enough unless the biggings were struck, it was the horses she'd to think of.

Right athwart her vision the haystacks shone up like great pointed pyramids a blinding moment, vanished, darkness complete and heavy flowed back on her again, the lantern-light seeking to pierce it like the bore of a drill. Still the rain held off as she stumbled and cried down the sodden fields. Then she saw that the barbed wire was alive, the lightning ran and glowed along it, a living thing, a tremulous, vibrant serpent that spat and glowed and hid its head and quivered again to sight. If the horses stood anywhere near to that they were finished, she cried to them again and stopped and listened, it was deathly still in the night between the bursts of the thunder, so still that she heard the grass she had pressed underfoot crawl and quiver erect again a step behind her. Then, as the thunder moved away—it seemed to break and roar down the rightward hill, above the Manse and Kinraddie Mains—something tripped her, she fell and the lantern-flame flared up and seemed almost to vanish; but she righted it, almost sick though she was because of the wet, warm thing that her body and face lay upon.

It was old Bob, he lay dead, his tongue hanging out, his legs doubled under him queerly, poor brute, and she shook at his halter a minute before she realized it was useless and there were still Bess and Clyde to see to. And then she heard the thunder and clop of their hooves coming across the grass to her, they loomed suddenly into the light of the lamp, nearly running her down, they stood beside her and whinnied, frightened and quivering so that her hand on Bess's neck dirled as on the floor of a threshing-machine.

Then the lightning smote down again, quite near, though the thunder had seemed to move off, it played a great zig-zag over the field where she stood with the horses, and they pressed so near her she was almost crushed between them; and the lantern was pressed from her hand at last, it fell and went out with a crash and a crinkle of breaking glass. She caught Bess's bridle with one hand, Clyde's with another, and the lightning went and they began to move forward in the darkness, she thought she was in the right direction but she couldn't be sure. The next flash showed a field she didn't know, close at hand, with a high staked dyke, and then she knew she had gone utterly wrong, it was the dyke on the turnpike.

The thunder growled satisfiedly and Clyde whinnied and whinnied, she saw then the reason for that, right ahead was the waving of a lantern, it must be Uncle come out to look for her at last, she cried *I'm here*! and a voice cried *Where*? She cried again and the lantern came in her direction, it was two men climbing the dyke. The horses started and whinnied and dragged her forward and then she found herself with Chae Strachan and Ewan, they had seen to their own horses on Upperhill and the Knapp, and had met and had minded hers on Blawearie; and up they had come to look for them. In the moment as they recognized one the other the lightning flared, a last sizzling glow, and then the rain came again, they heard it coming far up in the moors, it whistled and moaned and then was a great driving swish. Chae thrust his lantern upon Ewan, *Damn't man, take that and the lass and run for the house! I'll see to the horses!*

*from* SUNSET SONG

# NEIL MUNRO

## THE LOST PIBROCH

· · ✳ · ·

To the make of a piper go seven years of his own learning and seven generations before. If it is in, it will out, as the Gaelic old-word says; if not, let him take to the net or sword. At the end of his seven years one born to it will stand at the start of knowledge, and leaning a fond ear to the drone he may have parley with old folks of old affairs. Playing the tune of the 'Fairy Harp', he can hear his forefolks, plaided in skins, towsy-headed and terrible, grunting at the oars and snoring in the caves; he has his whittle and club in the 'Desperate Battle' (my own tune, my darling!), where the white-haired sea-rovers are on the shore, and a stain's on the edge of the tide; or, trying his art at Laments, he can stand by the cairn of kings, ken the colour of Fingal's hair, and see the moon-glint on the hook of the Druids!

Today there are but three pipers in the wide world, from the Sound of Sleat to the Wall of France. Who they are, and what their tartan, it is not for one to tell who has no heed for a thousand dirks in his doublet, but they may be known by the lucky ones who hear them. Namely players tickle the chanter and take out but the sound; the three give a tune the charm that I mention—a long thought and a bard's thought, and they bring the notes from the deeps of time, and the tale from the heart of the man who made it.

But not of the three best in Albainn today is my story, for they have not the Lost Pibroch. It is of the three best, who were not bad, in a place I ken—Half Town that stands in the wood.

You may rove for a thousand years on league-long brogues, or

hurry on fairy wings from isle to isle and deep to deep, and find
no equal to that same Half Town. It is not the splendour of it, nor
the riches of its folk; it is not any great routh of field or sheepfank,
but the scented winds of it, and the comfort of the pine-trees
round and about it on every hand. My mother used to be saying
(when I had the notion of fairy tales), that once on a time, when
the woods were young and thin, there was a road through them,
and the pick of children of a country-side wandered among them
into this place to play at sheilings. Up grew the trees, fast and
tall, and shut the little folks in so that the way out they could
not get if they had the mind for it. But never an out they wished
for. They grew with the firs and alders, a quiet clan in the heart
of the big wood, clear of the world out-by.

But now and then wanderers would come to Half Town,
through the gloomy coves, under the tall trees. There were
pack-men with tales of the out-world. There were broken men
flying from rope or hatchet. And once on a day of days came two
pipers—Gilian, of Clan Lachlan of Strathlachlan, and Rory Ban,
of the Macnaghtons of Dundarave. They had seen Half Town
from the sea—smoking to the clear air on the hillside; and through
the weary woods they came, and the dead quiet of them, and they
stood on the edge of the fir-belt.

Before them was what might be a township in a dream, and
to be seen at the one look, for it stood on the rising hill that
goes back on Lochow.

The dogs barked, and out from the houses and in from the
fields came the quiet clan to see who could be there. Biggest of
all the men, one they named Coll, cried on the strangers to
come forward; so out they went from the wood-edge, neither
coy nor crouse, but the equal of friend or foe, and they passed the
word of day.

'Hunting,' they said, 'in Easachosain, we found the roe come
this way.'

'If this way she came, she's at Duglas Water by now, so you

may bide and eat. Few, indeed, come calling on us in Half Town;
but whoever they are, here's the open door, and the horn spoon,
and the stool by the fire.'

He took them in and he fed them, nor asked their names nor
calling, but when they had eaten well he said to Rory, 'You
have skill of the pipes; I know by the drum of your fingers on
the horn spoon.'

'I have tried them,' said Rory, with a laugh, 'a bit—a bit. My
friend here is a player.'

'You have the art?' asked Coll.

'Well, not what you might call the whole art,' said Gilian,
'but I can play—oh yes! I can play two or three ports.'

'You can that!' said Rory.

'No better than yourself, Rory.'

'Well, maybe not, but—anyway, not all tunes; I allow you do
"Mackay's Banner" in pretty style.'

'Pipers,' said Coll, with a quick eye to a coming quarrel, 'I
will take you to one of your own trade in this place—Paruig Dall,
who is namely for music.'

'It's a name that's new to me,' said Rory, short and sharp, but
up they rose and followed Big Coll.

He took them to a bothy behind the Half Town, a place with
turf walls and never a window, where a blind man sat winding
pirns for weaver-folks.

'This,' said Coll, showing the strangers in at the door, 'is a
piper of parts, or I'm no judge, and he has as rare a stand of great
pipes as ever my eyes sat on.'

'I have that same,' said the blind man, with his face to the door.
'Your friends, Coll?'

'Two pipers of the neighbourhood,' Rory made answer. 'It
was for no piping we came here, but by the accident of the chase.
Still and on, if pipes are here, piping there might be.'

'So be it,' cried Coll; 'but I must go back to my cattle till
night comes. Get you to the playing with Paruig Dall, and I'll

find you here when I come back.'And with that he turned about and went off.

Paruig put down the ale and cake before the two men, and 'Welcome you are,' said he.

They ate the stranger's bite, and lipped the stranger's cup, and then, 'Whistle "The Macraes' March", my fair fellow,' said the blind man.

'How ken you I'm fair?' asked Rory.

'Your tongue tells that. A fair man has aye a soft bit in his speech, like the lapping of milk in a cogie; and a black one, like your friend there, has the sharp ring of a thin burn in frost running into an iron pot. "The Macraes' March", *laochain*.[1]'

Rory put a pucker on his mouth and played a little of the fine tune.

'So!' said the blind man, with his head to a side, 'you had your lesson. And you, my Strathlachlan boy without beard, do you ken "Muinntir a' Ghlinne so"?'

'How ken ye I'm Strathlachlan and beardless?' asked Gilian.

'Strathlachlan by the smell of herring-scale from your side of the house (for they told me yesterday the gannets were flying down Strathlachlan way, and that means fishing), and you have no beard I know, but in what way I know I do not know.'

Gilian had the *siubhal*[2] of the pibroch but begun when the blind man stopped him.

'You have it,' he said, 'you have it in a way, the Macarthur's way, and that's not my way. But, no matter, let us to our piping.'

The three men sat them down on three stools on the clay floor, and the blind man's pipes passed round between them.

'First,' said Paruig (being the man of the house, and to get the vein of his own pipes)—'first I'll put on them "The Vaunting".' He stood to his shanks, a lean old man and straight, and the big drone came nigh on the black rafters, He filled the bag at a breath and swung a lover's arm round about it. To those who

[1] hero        [2] allegro

know not the pipes, the feel of the bag in the oxter is a gaiety lost. The sweet round curve is like a girl's waist; it is friendly and warm in the crook of the elbow and against a man's side, and to press it is to bring laughing or tears.

The bothy roared with the tuning, and then the air came melting and sweet from the chanter. Eight steps up, four to the turn, and eight down went Paruig, and the *piobaireachd*[1] rolled to his fingers like a man's rhyming. The two men sat on the stools, with their elbows on their knees, and listened.

He played but the *urlar*,[2] and the *crunluadh*[3] to save time, and he played them well.

'Good indeed! Splendid, my old fellow!' cried the two; and said Gilian, 'You have a way of it in the crunluadh not my way, but as good as ever I heard.'

'It is the way of Padruig Og,' said Rory. 'Well I know it! There are tunes and tunes, and "The Vaunting" is not bad in its way, but give me "The Macraes' March".'

He jumped to his feet and took the pipes from the old man's hands, and over his shoulder with the drones.

'Stand back, lad!' he cried to Gilian, and Gilian went nearer the door.

The march came fast to the chanter—the old tune, the first tune that Kintail has heard before, when the wild men in their red tartan came over hill and moor; the tune with the river in it, the fast river and the courageous that kens not stop nor tarry, that runs round rock and over fall with good humour, yet no mood for anything but the way before it; the tune of the heroes, the tune of the pinelands and the broad straths, the tune that makes the eagles of Loch Duich crack their beaks together when they hear, and the crows of that countryside would as soon listen to as the squeal of their babies.

'Well! mighty well!' said Paruig Dall. 'You have the tartan of the clan in it.'

[1] symphony          [2] melody          [3] movement

'Not bad, I'll allow,' said Gilian. 'Let me try.'

He put his fingers on the holes, and his heart took a leap back over two generations, and yonder was Glencoe! The grey day crawled on the white hills and the black roofs smoked below. Snow choked the pass, eas[1] and corri filled with drift and flatted to the brae-face; the wind tossed quirky and cruel in the little bushes and among the smooring lintels and joists; and the blood of old and young lappered on the hearthstone. Out of the place went the tramped path of the Campbell butchers—far on their way to Glenlyon and the towns of paper and ink and liars— 'Muinntir a' ghlinne so, muinntir a' ghlinne so!—People, people, people of this glen, this glen, this glen!'

'Dogs! dogs! O God of grace—dogs and cowards!' cried Rory. 'I could be dirking a Diarmaid[2] or two if by luck they were near me.'

'It is piping that is to be here,' said Paruig, 'and it is not piping for an hour nor piping for an evening, but the piping of Dunvegan that stops not for sleep nor supper.'

So the three stayed in the bothy and played tune about while time went by the door. The birds flew home to the branches, the long-necked beasts flapped off to the shore to spear their flat fish; the rutting deers bellowed with loud throats in the deeps of the wood that stands round Half Town, and the scents of the moist night came gusty round the door. Over the back of Auchnabreac the sun trailed his plaid of red and yellow, and the loch stretched salt and dark from Cairn Dubh of Creaggans.

In from the hill the men and women came, weary-legged, and the bairns nodded at their heels. Sleepiness was on the land, but the pipers, piping in the bothy, kept the world awake.

'We will go to bed in good time,' said the folks, eating their suppers at their doors; 'in good time when the tune is ended.' But tune came on tune, and every tune better than its neighbour, and they waited.

[1] cataract          [2] Campbell

A cruisie-light was set alowe in the blind man's bothy, and the three men played old tunes and new tunes—salute and lament and brisk dances and marches that coax tired brogues on the long roads.

'Here's "Tulloch Ard" for you, and tell me who made it,' said Rory.

'Who kens that? Here's "Raasay's Lament", the best port Padruig Mor ever put together.'

'Tunes and tunes. I'm for "A Kiss o' the King's Hand".'

> *'Thug mi pòg 'us pòg 'us pòg,*
> *Thug mi pòg do làmh an righ,*
> *Cha do chuir gaoth an craicionn caorach,*
> *Fear a fhuair an fhaoilt ach mil'*

Then a quietness came on Half Town, for the piping stopped, and the people at their doors heard but their blood thumping and the night-hags in the dark of the fir-wood.

'A little longer and maybe there will be more,' they said to each other, and they waited; but no more music came from the drones, so they went in to bed.

There was a quiet over Half Town, for the three pipers talked about the Lost Tune.

'A man my father knew,' said Gilian, 'heard a bit of it once in Moideart. A terrible fine tune he said it was, but sore on the mind.'

'It would be the tripling,' said the Macnaghton, stroking a reed with a fond hand.

'Maybe. Tripling is ill enough, but what is tripling? There is more in piping than brisk fingers. Am I no right, Paruig?'

'Right, oh! right. The Lost Piobaireachd asks for skilly tripling, but Macruimen himself could not get at the core of it for all his art.'

'You have heard it then!' cried Gilian.

The blind man stood up and filled out his breast.

'Heard it!' he said; 'I heard it, and I play it—on the *feadan*[1], but not on the full set. To play the tune I mention on the full set is what I have not done since I came to Half Town.'

'I have ten round pieces in my sporran, and a bonnet-brooch it would take much to part me from; but they're there for the man who'll play me the Lost Piobaireachd,' said Gilian, with the words tripping each other to the tip of his tongue.

'And here's a Macnaghton's fortune on the top of the round pieces,' cried Rory, emptying his purse on the table.

The old man's face got hot and angry. 'I am not,' he said, 'a tinker's minstrel, to give my tuning for bawbees and a quaich of ale. The king himself could not buy the tune I ken if he had but a whim for it. But when pipers ask it they can have it, and it's yours without a fee. Still if you think to learn the tune by my piping once, poor's the delusion. It is not a port to be picked up like a cockle on the sand, for it takes the schooling of years and blindness forbye.'

'Blindness?'

'Blindness indeed. The thought of it is only for the dark eye.'

'If we could hear it on the full set!'

'Come out, then, on the grass, and you'll hear it, if Half Town should sleep no sleep this night.'

They went out of the bothy to the wet short grass. Ragged mists shook o'er Cowal, and on Ben Ime sat a horned moon like a galley of Lorn.

'I heard this tune from the Moideart man—the last in Albainn who knew it then, and he's in the clods,' said the blind fellow.

He had the mouthpiece at his lip, and his hand was coaxing the bag, when a bairn's cry came from a house in Half Town— a suckling's whimper, that, heard in the night, sets a man's mind busy on the sorrows that folks are born to. The drones clattered together on the piper's elbow and he stayed.

'I have a notion,' he said to the two men. 'I did not tell you

[1] chanter

that the Lost Piobaireachd is the piobaireachd of good-byes. It is the tune of broken clans, that sets the men on the foray and makes cold hearthstones. It was played in Glenshira when Gilleasbuig Gruamach could stretch stout swordsmen from Boshang to Ben Bhuidhe, and where are the folks of Glenshira this day? I saw a cheery night in Carnus that's over Lochow, and song and story busy about the fire, and the Moideart man played it for a wager. In the morning the weans were without fathers, and Carnus men were scattered about the wide world.'

'It must be the magic tune, sure enough,' said Gilian.

'Magic indeed, laochain! It is the tune that puts men on the open road, that makes restless lads and seeking women. Here's a Half Town of dreamers and men fattening for want of men's work. They forget the world is wide and roundabout their fir trees, and I can make them crave for something they cannot name.'

'Good or bad, out with it,' said Rory, 'if you know it at all.'

'Maybe no', maybe no'. I am old and done. Perhaps I have lost the right skill of the tune, for it's long since I put it on the great pipe. There's in me the strong notion to try it whatever may come of it, and here's for it.'

He put his pipe up again, filled the bag at a breath, brought the booming to the drones, and then the chanter-reed cried sharp and high.

'He's on it,' said Rory in Gilian's ear.

The groundwork of the tune was a drumming on the deep notes where the sorrows lie—'Come, come, come, my children, rain on the brae and the wind blowing.'

'It is a salute,' said Rory.

'It's the strange tune anyway,' said Gilian. 'Listen to the time of yon!'

The tune searched through Half Town and into the gloomy pine-wood; it put an end to the whoop of the night-hag and rang to Ben Bhreac. Boatmen deep and far on the loch could hear it, and Half Town folks sat up to listen.

Its story was the story that's ill to tell—something of the heart's longing and the curious chances of life. It bound up all the tales of all the clans, and made one tale of the Gaels' past. Dirk nor sword against the tartan, but the tartan against all else, and the Gaels' target fending the hill-land and the juicy straths from the pock-pitted little black men. The winters and the summers passing fast and furious, day and night roaring in the ears, and then again the clans at variance, and warders on every pass and on every parish.

Then the tune changed.

'Folks,' said the reeds, coaxing, 'wide's the world and merry the road. Here's but the old story and the women we kissed before. Come, come to the flat-lands rich and full, where the wonderful new things happen and the women's lips are still to try!'

'Tomorrow,' said Gilian in his friend's ear—'tomorrow I will go jaunting to the North. It has been in my mind since Beltane.'

'One might be doing worse,' said Rory, 'and I have the notion to try a trip with my cousin to the foreign wars.'

The blind piper put up his shoulder higher and rolled the air into the *crunluadh breabach*[1] that comes prancing with variations. Pride stiffened him from heel to hip, and hip to head, and set his sinews like steel.

He was telling of the gold to get for the searching and the bucks that may be had for the hunting. 'What,' said the reeds, 'are your poor crops, slashed by the constant rain and rotting, all for a scart in the bottom of a pot? What are your stots and heifers—black, dun, and yellow—to milch-cows and horses? Here's but the same for ever—toil and sleep, sleep and toil even on, no feud nor foray nor castles to harry—only the starved field and the sleeping moss. Let us to a brisker place! Over yonder

[1] smarter movement

· 167 ·

are the long straths and the deep rivers and townships strewn thick as your corn-rigs; over yonder's the place of the packmen's tales and the packmen's wares; steep we the withies and go!'

The two men stood with heads full of bravery and dreaming— men in carouse. 'This,' said they, 'is the notion we had, but had no words for it. It's a poor trade piping and eating and making amusement when one might be wandering up and down the world. We must be packing the haversacks.'

Then the *crunluadh mach*[1] came fast and furious on the chanter, and Half Town shook with it. It buzzed in the ear like flowers in the Honey Croft, and made commotion among the birds rocking on their eggs in the wood.

'So! so!' barked the *iolair*[2] on Craig-an-eas. 'I have heard it before it was an ill thing to be satisfied; in the morning I'll try the kids on Maamside, for the hares are wersh and tough.' 'Hearken, dear,' said the *londubh*.[3] 'I know now why my beak is gold; it is because I once ate richer berries than the whortle, and in season I'll look for them on the braes of Glenfinne.' 'Honk-unk,' said the fox, the cunning red fellow, 'am not I the fool to be staying on this little brae when I know so many roads elsewhere?'

And the people sitting up in their beds in Half Town moaned for something new. 'Paruig Dall is putting the strange tune on her there,' said they. 'What the meaning of it is we must ask in the morning, but *ochanoch*![4] it leaves one hungry at the heart.' And the gusty winds came snell from the north, and where the dark crept first the day made his first showing, so that Ben Ime rose black against a grey sky.

'That's the Lost Piobaireachd,' said Paruig Dall when the bag sunk on his arm.

And the two men looked at him in a daze.

Sometimes in the spring of the year the winds from Lorn have it their own way with the Highlands. They will come tearing

---

[1] faster movement      [2] eagle      [3] blackbird      [4] alas!

furious over the hundred hills, spurred the faster by the prongs of Cruachan and Dunchuach, and the large woods of home toss before them like corn before the hook. Up come the poor roots and over on their broken arms go the tall trees, and in the morning the deer will trot through new lanes cut in the forest.

A wind of that sort came on the full of the day when the two pipers were leaving Half Town.

'Stay till the storm is over,' said the kind folks; and 'Your bed and board are here for the pipers' forty days,' said Paruig Dall. But 'No' said the two; 'we have business that your pio-baireachd put us in mind of.'

'I'm hoping that I did not play yon with too much skill,' said the old man.

'Skill or no skill,' said Gilian, 'the like of yon I never heard. You played a port that makes poor enough all ports ever one listened to, and piping's no more for us wanderers.'

'Blessings with thee!' said the folks all, and the two men went down into the black wood among the cracking trees.

Six lads looked after them, and one said, 'It is an ill day for a body to take the world for his pillow, but what say you to following the pipers?'

'It might,' said one, 'be the beginning of fortune. I am weary enough of this poor place, with nothing about it but wood and water and tufty grass. If we went now, there might be gold and girls at the other end.'

They took crooks and bonnets and went after the two pipers. And when they were gone half a day, six women said to their men, 'Where can the lads be?'

'We do not know that,' said the men, with hot faces, 'but we might be looking.' They kissed their children and went, with cromags[1] in their hands, and the road they took was the road the King of Errin rides, and that is the road to the end of days.

A weary season fell on Half Town, and the very bairns dwined

[1] shepherds' crooks

at the breast for a change of fortune. The women lost their strength, and said, 'Today my back is weak, tomorrow I will put things to right,' and they looked slack-mouthed and heedless-eyed at the sun wheeling round the trees. Every week a man or two would go to seek something—a lost heifer or a wounded roe that was never brought back—and a new trade came to the place, the selling of herds. Far away in the low country, where the winds are warm and the poorest have money, black-cattle were wanted, so the men of Half Town made up long droves and took them round Glen Beag and the Rest.

Wherever they went they stayed, or the clans on the roadside put them to steel, for Half Town saw them no more. And a day came when all that was left in that fine place were but women and children and a blind piper.

'Am I the only man here?' asked Paruig Dall when it came to the bit, and they told him he was.

'Then here's another for fortune!' said he, and he went down through the woods with his pipes in his oxter.

# NEIL MUNRO

## THE VALENTINE THAT MISSED FIRE

. . * . .

A FORTNIGHT of strict teetotalism on the part of the Captain was too much of a joke for his crew. 'It's just bounce,' said the mate; 'he's showing off. I'm a Rechabite[1] for six years, every time I'm in Gleska; but I never let it put between me and a gless of good Brutish spurits wi' a shipmate in any port, Loch Fyne or foreign.'

[1] a member of a Temperance Society

'It's most annoyin',' said The Tar. 'He asked me yesterday if my health wassna breaking doon wi' drink, the same ass it would break doon wi' aal I take.'

'Chust what I told you; nothing but bounce!' said Dougie gloomily. 'Stop you! Next time he's in trum, I'll no' be so handy at pullin' corks for him. If I wass losin' my temper wi' him, I would give him a bit o' my mind.'

The engineer, wiping his brow with a wad of oily waste, put down the penny novelette he was reading and gave a contemptuous snort. 'I wonder to hear the two o' ye talkin',' said he. 'Ye're baith feared for him. I could soon fix him.'

'Could you, Macphail?' said Dougie. 'You're aawful game: what would you do?'

'I would send him a valentine that would vex him,' replied the engineer promptly; 'a fizzer o' a valentine that would mak' his hair curl for him.'

The mate impulsively smacked his thigh. 'My Chove! Macphail,' said he, 'it's the very ticket! What do you say to a valentine for the Captain, Colin?'

'Whatever you think yersel',' said The Tar.

That night Dougie and The Tar went ashore at Tarbert for a valentine. There was one shop-window up the town with a gorgeous display of penny 'mocks', designed and composed to give the recipient in every instance a dull, sickening thud on the bump of his self-esteem. The two mariners saw no valentine, however, that quite met the Captain's case.

'There'll be plenty o' other wans inside on the coonter,' said Dougie diplomatically. 'Away you in, Colin, and pick wan suitable, and I'll stand here and watch.'

'Watch what?' inquired The Tar suspiciously. 'It would be more like the thing if you went in and bought it yoursel'; I'll maybe no' get wan that'll please you.'

'Aal you need to ask for iss a mock valentine, lerge size and pretty broad, for a skipper wi' big feet. I would go in mysel' in a meenute if it wassna that—if it wassna that it would look droll, and me a muddle-aged man wi' whuskers.'

The Tar went into the shop reluctantly, and was horrified to find a rather pretty girl behind the counter. He couldn't for his life suggest mock valentines to her, and he could not with decency back out without explanation.

'Have you any—have you any nice unvelopes?' he inquired bashfully, as she stood waiting his order.

'What size?' she asked.

'Lerge size, and pretty broad, for a skipper wi' big feet,' said The Tar in his confusion. Then he corrected himself, adding, 'Any size, muss, suitable for holding letters.'

'There's a great run on that kind of envelope this winter,' the lady remarked, being a humorist. 'How many?'

'A ha'pennyworth,' said the Tar. 'I'll chust take them wi' me.'

When The Tar came out of the shop the mate was invisible, and it was only after some search he found him in a neighbouring public-house.

'I chust came in here to put by the time,' said Dougie; 'but seein' you're here, what am I for?'

The Tar, realizing that there must be an unpleasant revelation immediately, produced the essential threepence and paid for beer.

'I hope you got yon?' said the mate anxiously.

'Ass sure ass daith, Dougie, I didna like to ask for it,' explained the young man pathetically. 'There's a gasalier and two paraffin lamps bleezin' in the shop, and it would gie me a rud face to ask for a mock valentine in such an illumination. Iss there no other wee dark shop in the toon we could get what we want in?'

The mate surveyed him with a disgusted countenance. 'Man, you're a coward, Colin,' he said. 'The best in the land goes in and buys mock valentines, and it's no disgrace to nobody so long ass he has the money in his hand. If I had another gless o' beer I would go in mysel'.'

'You'll get that!' said The Tar gladly, and produced another threepence, after which they returned to the shop-window, where Dougie's courage apparently failed him, in spite of the extra glass of beer. 'It's no' that I give a docken for anybody,' he explained, 'but you see I'm that weel kent in Tarbert. What sort o' body keeps the shop?'

'Och, it's chust an old done man wi' a sore hand and wan eye no' neebours,' replied The Tar strategically. 'Ye needna be frightened for him; he'll no' say a cheep. To bleezes wi' him!'

Dougie was greatly relieved at this intelligence. 'Toots!' he said. 'Iss that aal? Watch me!' and he went banging in at the door in three strides.

The lady of the shop was in a room behind. To call her attention Dougie cried, 'Shop!' and kicked the front of the counter, with his eyes already on a pile of valentines ready for a rush of business in that elegant form of billet-doux. When the pretty girl came skipping out of the back room, he was even more astounded and alarmed than The Tar had been.

'A fine night,' he remarked affably; 'iss your faither at the back?'

'I think you must have made a mistake in the shop,' said the lady. 'Who do you want?'

'Him with the sore hand and the wan eye no' right neebours,' said the mate, not for a moment suspecting that The Tar had misled him. 'It's parteecular business; I'll no' keep him wan meenute.'

'There's nobody here but myself,' the girl informed him, and then he saw that he had been deceived by his shipmate.

'Stop you till I get that Tar!' he exclaimed with natural exasperation, and was on the point of leaving when the pile of valentines met his eye again, and he decided to brazen it out.

'Maybe you'll do yoursel',' said he, with an insinuating leer at the shopkeeper. 'There iss a shipmate o' mine standin' oot there took a kind o' notion o' a mock valentine and doesna like to ask for it. He wass in a meenute or two ago—you would know him by the warts on his hand—but he hadna the nerve to ask for it.'

'There you are, all kinds,' said the lady, indicating the pile on the counter, with a smile of comprehension. 'A penny each.'

Dougie wet his thumb and clumsily turned over the valentines, seeking for one appropriate to a sea captain silly enough to be teetotal. 'It's chust for a baur, mind you,' he explained to the lady. 'No herm at aal, at aal; chust a bit of a high jeenk. Forbye, it's no' for me: it's for the other fellow, and his name's Colin Turner, but he's blate, blate.' He raised his voice so that The Tar, standing outside the window, could hear him quite plainly; with the result that The Tar was so ashamed, he pulled down his cap on his face and hurriedly walked off to the quay.

'There's an awful lot o' them valentines for governesses and tylers and polismen,' said Dougie; 'the merchant service doesna get mich of a chance. Have you nothing smert and nippy that'll fit a sea captain, and him teetotal?'

The shopkeeper hurriedly went over her stock, and discovered that teetotalism was the one eccentricity valentines never dealt with; on the contrary, they were all for people with red noses and bibulous propensities.

'There's none for teetotal captains,' said she; 'but here's one for a captain that's not teetotal,' and she showed a valentine with a most unpleasant-looking seaman, in a state of intoxication, walking arm-in-arm with a respectable-looking young woman.

'Man, that's the very tup!' said Dougie, delighted. 'It's ass clever a thing ass ever I seen. I wonder the way they can put them valentines thegather. Read what it says below. I havena my specs.'

The shopkeeper read the verse on the valentine:

'The girl that would marry a man like you
Would have all the rest of her life to rue;
A sailor soaked in salt water and rum
Could never provide a happy home.'

'Capital!' exclaimed the mate, highly delighted. 'Ass smert ass anything in the works of Burns. That wan'll do splendid.'

'I thought it was for a teetotal captain you wanted one,' said the lady, as she folded up the valentine.

'He's only teetotal to spite us,' said Dougie. 'And that valentine fits him fine, for he's coortin' a baker's weedow, and he thinks we don't know. Mind you, it's no' me that's goin' to send the valentine, it's Colin Turner; but there's no herm, chust a bit of a baur. You ken yoursel'.'

Then an embarrasing idea occurred to him—who was to address the envelope?

'Do you keep mournin' unvelopes?' he asked.

'Black-edged envelopes—yes,' said the shopkeeper.

'Wan,' said Dougie; and when he got it he put the valentine inside and ventured to propose to the lady that, seeing she had pen and ink handy, she might address the envelope for him, otherwise the recipient would recognize Colin Turner's hand-of-write.

The lady obliged, and addressed the document to:

> Captain Peter Macfarlane,
> s.s. Vital Spark,
> Tarbert.

Dougie thanked her effusively on behalf of The Tar, paid for his purchases and a penny stamp, and went out. As he found his shipmate gone, he sealed the envelope and posted it.

When the letter-carrier came down Tarbert quay next morning, all the crew of the *Vital Spark* were on deck—the Captain in blissful unconsciousness of what was in store for him, the others anxious not to lose the expression of his countenance when he should open his valentine.

It was a busy day on the *Vital Spark*; all hands had to help to get in a cargo of wood.

'A mournin' letter for you, Captain,' said the letter-carrier, handing down the missive.

Para Handy looked startled, and walked aft to open it. He took one short but sufficient glimpse at the valentine, with a suspicious glance at the crew, who were apparently engrossed in admiration of the scenery round Tarbert. Then he went down the fo'c'sle, to come up a quarter of an hour later with his good clothes on, his hat, and a black tie.

'What the duvvle game iss he up to noo?' said Dougie, greatly astonished.

'I hope it didna turn his brain,' said The Tar. 'A fright sometimes does it. Wass it a very wild valentine, Dougie?'

Para Handy moved aft with a sad, resigned aspect, the mourning envelope in his hand. 'I'm sorry I'll have to go away till the efternoon, boys,' he said softly. 'See and get in that wud nice and smert before I come back.'

'What's wrong?' asked Dougie, mystified.

The Captain ostentatiously blew his nose, and explained that they might have noticed he had just got a mourning letter.

'Was't a mournin' wan? I never noticed,' said Dougie.

'Neither did I,' added The Tar hurriedly.

'Yes,' said the Captain sadly, showing them the envelope; 'my poor cousin Cherlie over in Dunmore iss no more; he just slipped away yesterday, and I'm goin' to take the day off and make arrangements.'

'Well, I'm jiggered!' exclaimed Dougie, as they watched Para Handy walking off on what was to be a nice holiday at their expense, for they would now have his share of the day's work to do as well as their own.

'Did you ever see such a nate liar?' said The Tar, lost in admiration at the cunning of the Captain.

And then they fell upon the engineer, and abused him for suggesting the valentine.

*from* PARA HANDY AND OTHER TALES

# NEIL M. GUNN

## DEATH OF THE LAMB

.. * ..

As he approached the solitary elm in the upland field of the large
glen farm, his eye was caught by the flight of a grey crow from
its upper branches. His mind quickened sharply for he did not
like the bird; his eyes narrowed as they followed the watchful
sideways flight, the careless haphazard on-flying that was always
so sinister; then they dropped to search around and saw the
full-grown lamb in the long grass of the ditch.

He came within a few feet of it and stopped. A round hole
over two inches deep and about an inch across had been eaten
out of its right flank. The hole was red but no blood flowed from
it. The lamb swayed very slightly on its legs, its eyes were inclined
to close and its ears to droop.

The man was seized with a strong revulsion of feeling, with a
hatred of the loathsome grey-black bird, with anger, and also
with a desire to walk away, for he could do nothing. There was
no one anywhere to be seen; no one who had seen him. Even the
crow had vanished. He took a few steps downward and paused,
for as surely as he went on would the crow return and continue
its ghastly meal. The earth around him caught the dark silence of a
battlefield.

He went back to the lamb and stared at it, stooped to stare into
the red hole, at the intermittent quiver that went over the flesh,
at the half-closed eyes, at the head drooping towards fatal sleep.
It seemed quite unaware of him. Death wasn't far off—yet the
brute was still on its legs, might endure like this for hours,
perhaps a whole night, and its eyelids would continue to flicker

down to defeat the beak that liked to peck the eyeball as a titbit.

He glanced about the grass, looking for a stone or a stick. There was neither. One sharp blow on the forehead and all would be over. But it was not his lamb. There was nothing he could properly do about it except walk away and report the matter to the shepherd should he happen to come across him. So he set off, leaving the lamb swaying in the tall grass, lifting an eye to watch for the crow, with bitter anger in his mind and a queer undefined hatred. Once he cleared his throat and spat, but that did not cleanse his mouth.

Soon he felt he must find the shepherd, and when he saw the farm workers harvesting a field, he went through the wire fence and strolled over towards them. Yes, there was the shepherd helping with the stooking, and he knew at once a sharp sense of relief. When he had told the shepherd, his responsibility would end.

'Come to give us a hand?' the shepherd greeted him cheerfully.

The man returned the sally and after they had chatted about the good crop said: 'By the way, there's a lamb of yours up there on its last legs. A crow was pecking a hole in its flank. It's still standing.'

'Oh,' said the shepherd, and looked at him.

'I didn't know what to do about it, so thought I'd come and tell you.'

'I see,' said the shepherd, looking away. Then he picked up a couple of sheaves and set them leaning against each other. 'It seems he's done for in that case.'

'Yes.'

The shepherd picked up another couple of sheaves, and then paused. There obviously wasn't much that he could do about it. He seemed reluctant to leave the field. 'I had one that went like that last week.' He walked away a few paces and came back with another two sheaves.

'I felt like putting it out of its misery, but I didn't know what to do, so I thought I'd tell you,' said the man, looking at the other workers.

When the shepherd had completed his stook of eight sheaves, he paused again. 'Is it far up?'

'Not very. Just up at the elm tree. I don't suppose there's much you can do for it.'

'No,' said the shepherd in a flat voice; then he began to move over to his black jacket which lay against a stook. When the shepherd had his jacket on, they started walking across to the fence. The shepherd took out his pipe and paused to light its already half-consumed tobacco. 'When they get that trouble on them, there's nothing can be done.'

He felt that the shepherd now had a grudge against him, and this embarrassed him. There was nothing a man could do. He should have left the shepherd alone, instead of coming like a sensitive woman to tell what he had seen. But he answered in his normal voice, and the shepherd spoke calmly. Yes, there were showers, but the wind soon dried everything up. It was good enough harvest weather.

As they approached the elm-tree, two crows got up and flapped away. 'Ugly brutes,' said the shepherd, and then, going forward, he stood before the lamb.

It was still on its legs, swaying very slightly, shivering now and then, its eyelids half-closed, its head drooping. The shepherd squatted down and peered at the bloody hole; then remained squatting for a long time apparently lost in contemplation of the lamb.

He got up with an odd and distant air. In a voice dry and practical, he said, 'No, there's nothing can be done now, nothing but the one thing.' He looked at the tree and abroad over the bare upland pasture. 'You need a licence to kill a beast these days,' he said with a humour in which there was no stress. Then he took out his pocket-knife and opened the big blade.

'Well,' he greeted the lamb, patting it gently on the back. 'It will be all right now, all right.' He got his left hand across the throat. The lamb struggled. 'It's all right,' murmured the shepherd soothingly, 'all right,' as if talking to a fevered child, and now with all his strength he was getting at the bone. The vertebrae snapped, and the shepherd severed the spinal cord which then showed between the bone joints like two ends of white tape. He dropped the lamb. The body continued to jerk convulsively.

The shepherd cleaned the blade of his knife by stabbing it in the grass. Then he gave it a final wipe against his trousers.

'It's a job I hate,' he said in his calm voice as he clicked the blade shut.

'Well, I'm glad it's out of its misery, anyway,' said the man as lightly as he could.

They returned, as they had come up, talking in even friendly tones, but when the shepherd left him the man felt that in some way he had been a soft fool. Also there was somehow in the air a feeling of misery, of guilt. The shadow of the whole business had not only come between the shepherd and himself, but between himself and everything. It attached itself to his clothes and to the trees, and the grey crows flew through it.

*from* HIGHLAND PACK

# DAVID STEPHEN

## BRIGHT EYES

. . * . .

ACROSS the wind-ruffled surface of the loch a silver pathway led away to the moon, and the shining water was pencilled with shadows which were ripples curling inshore. Through the sere, whispering threshes in the shallows thin ice crept out to meet the lap of water. The pines crowding down to the east shore were hard and black against the moon. Ducks dozed unseen in the ripple shadows—mallard and goldeneye, teal, tufted and shoveler; and grey geese slept a waking sleep, fearing the otter they had seen on the shore at the going down of the sun. A barn owl, flying over the loch twelve feet over his shadow saw the otter dive where the pines made the water dark, and skirled his wild lament as he wafted overhead on wings as noiseless as sleep.

The otter swam inshore under his own moon-sparkling bubble chain, to hide in the reeds till lifted heads went down again. He was hungry after a day's fasting. There were no fish in the loch and he could not hope to reach the river till the following day.So he was prepared to try his luck at sleeping duck. Near the bank he paused, listening, with chin on rump and rudder coiled round his breast. His lack-lustre, water-dimmed eyes glared savagely and his fur was oil-sleek in the moonshine. He left the water as the barn owl flapped along the shore. On the point of snarling at the ghostly bird, he spun round with a grimace and a twitch of whiskers when his nose found the taint of fox. Out of the shadow of a blaeberry-cushioned hillock, faced with white, lit hummel ruub, came a big fox with a gigantic brush and teeth flashing pearl-white in the moonlight.

With the wind in his favour, the fox had early warning of the otter's presence, while his own was unsuspected. And he came prepared to chop. But when he saw the size of the otter he slowed at once to a dignified walk and veered away, trying to look unconcerned. The otter sat for a fraction of a second with one forepaw uplifted, and his lips drawn so far back from his teeth that the skin folds almost hid his eyes. Then he twisted away into the reeds, his entry betrayed by the twinkle of the shattering ice-film. For some moments he crouched among the broken reeds, with only his eyes and nostrils above the water, while the fox stood rigid. When the fox moved away he swam into deeper water and disappeared.

String Lug walked leisurely towards the dark pine strip, his pads making scarcely a whisper on the frosted grass.

A tawny owl hooted as he entered the strip. She left her perch, wicking wheezily when she saw the fox, and crossed the moon's face when she topped the trees. String Lug saw her silhouetted against the moon, big-headed and front-heavy, mewing like a cat till she pitched in another tree farther down the woodside. He stood like an image while she hooted from her new perch—a long-drawn-out, catenated, bubbling cry, which was the very voice of the solitude. How well he knew that cry! He had heard it almost nightly throughout his life, but on that night it made him feel at home.

In the moon-misted gloom, gold and green lights, which were the eyes of sheep, flashed on and off, and he heard the thud of hooves in flight. Pigeons, crows, and pheasants shuffled on perches above his head, but no bird took the air at his passing.

On the east side of the wood was a thick hedge, hiding the fence which topped the bank. From the deepest part of the hedge, where briars sent tendrils over the top, twin crimson stars flickered suddenly. The stars kept even eye-distance apart and held steady at fox height. The lights flashed off when String Lug minced forward, and he heard the rustle of a leaf touched by a hasty foot. The smell of the dog fox sent an electric shock through him. Rushing to the spot, he burst into the thorn tangle and sniffed at the soiling. When he pushed through into the open he was set for war.

Ere his brush was quite clear of the dragging thorns he stopped short, with head down and lips lifted. With eyes flaming green in the full glare of the moon, he pondered the strange spectacle before him. Fifty yards away, in a mossy depression between high peat banks, three dog foxes were walking in circles, with brushes rigid, rumps arched and heads askew. The bruses of all three were up and String Lug could see, every now and again, the fleeting flash of ivory. It was the first time he had seen such a party; but he knew it was a mating brawl and that somewhere not very far away would be the vixen over which they were arguing.

In his own veins the fire kindled quickly to fighting heat. Eager to miss nothing of the spectacle, he leaned forward into the wind like a dog feeling for the scent of a hidden bird. Suddenly he relaxed and sat down on his hunkers, to reflect on his mode of entry into the drama. He had the advantage of being on the wrong side of the wind for the others to smell him, so he had some little time in which to make up his mind.

As if at a prearranged signal the foxes stopped circling and rushed at each other in a mad scramble. String Lug heard a double yap, the quick intake of breath and the sudden gasp of air expelled by the shock of bodies. Brushes swiped wildly at eyes. Teeth flashed and clicked and foxes spat hair, while their musk scent came stronger to String Lug's nostrils. The smallest beast fell while the other two reared and met forepaws to forepaws and teeth to teeth. They made much show of worrying without unduly disturbing each other's whiskers, for they were not yet in really savage mood and had little stomach for a serious grapple. But they were warming up to it. String Lug knew they were fanning hate and courage and that soon their cut-and-run thrusts, their heel-nipping and eye-wiping, would give way to more serious fighting, unless two of them quit before then. He decided the moment had come to intervene.

He crawled to the edge of the peat bank without being seen, and grinned. He could smell the vixen beyond the opposite bank. The wind combed the fur of his ruff, shedding it like corn falling before a reaper. He rose when the foxes joined in another general mix-up. Pointing his nose to the sky he barked—three harsh yaps which ripped the air and froze the brawling foxes in their tracks. Their breath hung in puffs of white vapour above their heads, and their hanging tongues drooled warm sweat. The vixen squalled and String Lug leaped, and the moon smiled sardonically down.

The encounter was brief, the action swift, and String Lug was touching noses with the vixen before the dog foxes had time to pull in their tongues. He laid open the mask of one with a lightning slash of teeth, shouldered the smallest beast, which was a mangy cur with bare, dry patches on thighs and flanks, and walloped the third hard across the face with his gritty brush. Before they could unite against him, he was up the opposite bank and whimpering to the vixen where she sat in deep heather, chewing the fleshy thigh bone of a water-hen. She clicked her incisor teeth at him, parted her lips and snarled at him through locked molars. String Lug cringed, turning his face side on to her, expecting a nip in the cheek or a puncture in his upright ear. Instead, he heard the clash of teeth at his big tendon, and wheeled to meet the assault. It was the fox whose eyes he had wiped a few moments before.

String Lug's turn and counter-attack were carried through in one perfectly timed movement and his teeth scored a red furrow on the other's cheek. The beast danced back with a startled yelp, twisted away, and fled with rump down and brush curled under his belly. The others, coming in on a converging run to the assault, drew back when he reached at them with teeth bared and brush gathered for hitting. They bolted ignominiously in opposite directions, making as much noise as a duck pattering on mud. When String Lug turned back the vixen was already loping across the heather, a grey, gliding shape in the unclouded moonshine.

Throughout the night String Lug pursued and wooed her, skirmishing incessantly with two foxes which had still some courage left for arguing. One of them was the mangy dog who, like so many with similar afflictions, was a most persistent suitor. String Lug left him with several additional bare patches not caused by mange. By daylight he had won the battle and the lady. His bad temper vanished and the ache in his heart was stilled. And when the sun rose at last, sending waves of palest pink, washing over the barred lilac and saffron of the morning sky, he lay down beside her in a grouse butt and licked her willing ears.

*from* STRING LUG THE FOX

## ROBERT KEMP

### MACGURK AND THE BULL

· · * · ·

A HERD of black cattle was being shifted from one field into another, which meant that about fifty yards of the highway were obstructed by their lumbering shapes. They seemed by their glossy and substantial appearance to be prize beasts, and well they knew it, for their rate of process was a regal half a mile an hour, with occasional stops to eat a mouthful of the succulent green grass growing in the ditch by the roadside. A rough sort of points duty was being carried out by the farmer and two of his helpers. Their guiding principle seemed to be the cows first and the rest nowhere.

At first I halted with the patient courtesy of the veteran motorist, but on taking stock of the situation I noted that the herd seemed to be about a hundred strong and only at the beginning of its hegira. At the present rate of knots I estimated that the last of them would be clear in about half-an-hour. So, putting man before the animal creation, I began to edge forward, giving the horn an occasional peep-peep to warn the brutes to keep their distance.

Results were instantaneous, but unforeseen. One cow, which had been browsing in the ditch as if MacGurk's time did not possess any value, leapt half its height in the air and stampeded. At this another particularly large and somnolent animal turned its head and glowered at us. By the ring on its nose, as well as by other characteristics which I had overlooked, I could tell that it was the bull, the husband and defender of his harem.

To judge by his glance and the light in his bleary eyes, the Ford saloon was not his favourite model, nor did he care for the moustache which was peering at him anxiously from over the wheel. Emitting a low bellow, he wheeled about with unlooked-for agility, lowered his battering-ram of a brow and set about us. His females, of course, were in a state of wild excitement over the brave boyo, bellowing and running hither and thither. Dogs were barking and men shouting.

Where it might have ended no one could tell. Luckily, a wizened, intrepid, little fellow in dungarees rushed forward with a short stave which had a metal hook fixed to the end of it. I expect he was one of that strange and specialist race which spends all its life looking after bulls. At any rate, he expertly clicked the hook over the ring in the professional parent's nose and began to give it the works. In no time two tons of prime beef was whimpering for mercy and was led firmly away. The cows fell meekly into line astern.

I indignantly got out to inspect the damage. One of the wings was dented and a headlamp smashed to smithereens. By this time the farmer himself had come running up, waving an ashplant at me and purple in the face with fury. In build he somewhat resembled his own bull—not, I mean, in that he was fat, but in being extraordinarily thick in all his features and limbs.

'Ye — — — —,' he began. 'What the deil dae ye mean by toot-tootin' at my beasts wi' your horn and flegging them?'

I cautioned him rather sharply to mind his language, as there were ladies present.

'Ladies!' quoth he. 'Every coo in yon herd's a lady compared wi' the twa sulky-faced    s you have there in the back!'

I was within a hair's breadth of knocking him down, but remembered in time that the principal obligation upon an escort is to spare the ladies any scenes of naked violence.

'Look here,' I retorted, 'cut out the vulgar abuse. Do you see this car? I'm afraid your animal has damaged it severely.'

'Ach!' said the farmer, with a sad note in his voice. 'You can easy get another car like that at the nearest motor shop. But where-ever would I get another bull like Progenitor of Balmullo?'

'That's neither here nor there,' I replied. 'Unless you make good the damage to this car, I'll take you to court. Supply me with your name and address, if you please!'

'Nae bother about that,' said our opponent, fishing out the dirty envelope of some invoice or other, and handing it to MacGurk. 'While I'm about it, I'll just tak' yours, for if there's sae much as a scratch on Progenitor of Balmullo, it'll cost ye a thousand pounds!'

*from* THE CAMPAIGNS OF CAPTAIN MACGURK

# NOTES ON THE AUTHORS

ALLAN JOHN R : Born 1906. Writer and broadcaster. His works include—Farmer's Boy · North-east Lowlands · Down on the Farm.

BLAKE GEORGE : Born Greenock, 1893. Author and journalist. His works include—Sea Tangle · Rest and Be Thankful · The Shipbuilders · The Constant Star · Mountain and Flood · The Firth of Clyde · The Voyage Home · The Last Fling.

BORTHWICK ALASTAIR : Born 1913. Author and broadcaster. His works include—Always a Little Further.

BOSWELL JAMES : Born Edinburgh, 1740. Biographer of Dr. Johnson. His works include—Journal of a Tour to the Hebrides · A Life of Dr. Johnson.

BROGAN COLM : Born 1902. Journalist. His works include—Who Are The People? · The Democrat at the Supper Table · Our New Masters · Fifty Years On · The Glasgow Story.

BROWN JOHN : Born 1810. Writer and physician. His works include—Rab and his Friends · Horae Subsecivae.

BUCHAN JOHN : Born 1875. First Baron Tweedsmuir. Administrator and writer. His works include—Prester John · The Thirty-nine Steps · Huntingtower · The Three Hostages · Greenmantle · John Macnab · Biographies of Sir Walter Raleigh, Montrose, Sir Walter Scott, and Augustus.

CRONIN ARCHIBALD J : Born 1896. Novelist and physician. His works include—Hatter's Castle · The Stars Look Down · The Citadel · The Keys of the Kingdom · The Green Years · The Spanish Gardener · Adventures in Two Worlds · Beyond this Place.

CUNNINGHAM ALLAN : Born Keir, Dumfriesshire, 1784. Best known for his poetry. His prose works include—Lives of Eminent British Painters.

DARLING F FRASER : Born 1903. Writer and biologist. His works include—A Herd of Red Deer · A Naturalist on Rona · Island

Years · The Story of Scotland · Island Farm · Natural History in the Highlands and Islands · Report of the West Highland Survey.

DUNNETT ALASTAIR M : Born 1908. His works include—Treasure at Sonnach · Heard Tell · Quest by Canoe · Highlands and Islands of Scotland.

FINDLATER JANE H : Born Edinburgh, 1866. Her works include—Green Graves of Balgowrie · A Daughter of Strife · Rachel · Seven Scots Stories · A Green Grass Widow.

GIBBON LEWIS GRASSIC (James Leslie Mitchell) : Born, Hill of Seggat, Aberdeenshire, 1901. Author and archaeologist. His works include—Hanno or the Future of Exploration · Stained Radiance · The Conquest of the Maya · Sunset Song · Cloud Howe · Grey Granite · Niger: the life of Mungo Park.

GORDON SETON : Born 1886. Author and naturalist. His works include—Birds of the Loch and Mountain · The Charm of the Hills · Islands of the West · Highways and Byways in the Central Highlands · Golden Eagle, King of Birds.

GUNN NEIL M : Born 1891, on the Caithness coast. Writer. His works include —Grey Coast · Morning Tide · Highland River · The Silver Darlings · Young Art and Old Hector · The Serpent · The Drinking Well · The Atom of Delight · Highland Pack · Off in a Boat · The White Hour.

HANLEY CLIFFORD : Born Gallowgate, Glasgow, 1922. Journalist. His works include—Dancing in the Streets · newspaper articles.

HOGG JAMES : Born 1770, Ettrick, Selkirkshire. Poet known as the Ettrick Shepherd. His works include—The Mountain Bard · The Queen's Wake.

KEMP ROBERT : Born Longhope, Orkney, 1908. Novelist and playwright. His works include—The Highlander · The Malacca Cane · The MacGurk series.

LANG JOHN and JEAN : John Lang was born in 1849. Jean was his cousin and wife. Their works include—Land of Romance · Stories of the Border Marches.

LAUDER SIR THOMAS DICK : Born 1784. Novelist. His works include— Lochindhu · The Wolfe of Badenoch · Account of the Great Moray Floods · Highland Rambles and Legends · Legends and Tales of the Highlands.

LINKLATER ERIC : Born Orkney, 1899. Dramatist and novelist. His works include—Poet's Pub · Juan in America · Magnus Merriman · The Lion and the Unicorn · The Man on my Back · Socrates Asks Why · The Wind on the Moon · Private Angelo · Sealskin Trousers · Laxdale Hall · A Year of Space · The House of Gair.

McCRONE GUY : Born 1898. Novelist. His works include—Wax Fruit · Aunt Bel · The Hayburn Family.

MACKENZIE AGNES MURE : Born Stornoway, 1891. Historian and critic. Her works include—The Women in Shakespeare's Plays · The Process of Literature · Robert Bruce, King of Scots · I was at Bannockburn · Scotland in Modern Times · Scottish Pageant · The Kingdom of Scotland: a short history · Apprentice Majesty.

MACKENZIE ALEXANDER : Born 1838. His History of the Highland Clearances was published in Inverness in 1883.

McLAREN MORAY : Born Edinburgh, 1901. Author and journalist. His works include—Return to Scotland · The Highland Jaunt.

MILLER HUGH : Born Cromarty, 1802. Writer and geologist. His works include—Scenes and Legends of the North of Scotland · The Old Red Sandstone · Footprints of the Creator · My Schools and Schoolmasters.

MUIR EDWIN : Born Deerness, Orkney, 1887. Poet, journalist, critic, translator. His works include—Scottish Journey · The Story and the Fable · John Knox · Essays on Literature and Society · Scott and Scotland · The Three Brothers.

MUNRO NEIL : Born Inveraray, 1864. Author and journalist. His works include—John Splendid · The New Road · Doom Castle · The Daft Days · Fancy Farm · Children of Tempest · Gillian the Dreamer · Para Handy Tales · The Lost Pibroch.

POWER WILLIAM · Born Glasgow, 1873. Author and journalist. His works include—Pavement and Highway · The World Unvisited · Robert Burns and other Essays and Sketches · My Scotland · Scotland and the Scots · Prince Charlie.

SCOTT SIR WALTER : Born Edinburgh, 1771. Poet and novelist. His works include—Minstrelsy of the Scottish Border · Marmion · The Lady of the Lake · The Waverley Novels · A Life of Napoleon · Tales of a Grandfather.

SMITH ALEXANDER : Born Kilmarnock, 1830. Poet and essayist. His works include—A Summer in Skye · Alfred Hagert's Household · Miss Oona McQuarrie · Last Leaves.

STEPHEN DAVID : Born 1910. Writer and naturalist. His works include—String Lug · Six Pointer Buck · Days with the Golden Eagle · Getting to Know British Wild Animals.

STEVENSON ROBERT LOUIS : Born Edinburgh, 1850. Novelist and essayist. His works include—Familiar Studies of Men and Books · Virginibus Puerisque · An Inland Voyage · Travels With a Donkey · Treasure Island · Dr. Jekyll and Mr. Hyde · Kidnapped · The Master of Ballantrae · Catriona.